Race Relations

OPPOSING VIEWPOINTS®

Other Books of Related Interest

Race Relations

OPPOSING VIEWPOINTS®

James D. Torr, *Book Editor*

Bruce Glassman, *Vice President*
Bonnie Szumski, *Publisher*
Helen Cothran, *Managing Editor*

OPPOSING
VIEWPOINTS®
SERIES

GREENHAVEN PRESS
An imprint of Thomson Gale, a part of The Thomson Corporation

Detroit • New York • San Francisco • San Diego • New Haven, Conn.
Waterville, Maine • London • Munich

THOMSON
━━━━━★━━━━━ ™
GALE

LIBRARY OF CONGRESS CATALOGING-IN-PUBLICATION DATA

Race relations / James D. Torr, book editor.
    p. cm. — (Opposing viewpoints series)
Includes bibliographical references and index.
ISBN 0-7377-2955-4 (lib. : alk. paper) — ISBN 0-7377-2956-2 (pbk. : alk. paper)
    1. United States—Race relations. 2. Race discrimination—United States.
3. Racism—United States. 4. United States—Race relations—Government policy.
I. Torr, James D., 1974– . II. Opposing viewpoints series (Unnumbered)
E184.A1R316 2005
305.8'00973—dc22   2004059763

Printed in the United States of America

JUN - - 2006

"Congress shall make
no law...abridging the
freedom of speech, or of
the press."

First Amendment to the U.S. Constitution

The basic foundation of our democracy is the First
Amendment guarantee of freedom of expression.
The Opposing Viewpoints Series is dedicated to the
concept of this basic freedom and the idea that it is
more important to practice it than to enshrine it.

Contents

Why Consider Opposing Viewpoints?

"The only way in which a human being can make some approach to knowing the whole of a subject is by hearing what can be said about it by persons of every variety of opinion and studying all modes in which it can be looked at by every character of mind. No wise man ever acquired his wisdom in any mode but this."

John Stuart Mill

In our media-intensive culture it is not difficult to find differing opinions. Thousands of newspapers and magazines and dozens of radio and television talk shows resound with differing points of view. The difficulty lies in deciding which opinion to agree with and which "experts" seem the most credible. The more inundated we become with differing opinions and claims, the more essential it is to hone critical reading and thinking skills to evaluate these ideas. Opposing Viewpoints books address this problem directly by presenting stimulating debates that can be used to enhance and teach these skills. The varied opinions contained in each book examine many different aspects of a single issue. While examining these conveniently edited opposing views, readers can develop critical thinking skills such as the ability to compare and contrast authors' credibility, facts, argumentation styles, use of persuasive techniques, and other stylistic tools. In short, the Opposing Viewpoints Series is an ideal way to attain the higher-level thinking and reading skills so essential in a culture of diverse and contradictory opinions.

In addition to providing a tool for critical thinking, Opposing Viewpoints books challenge readers to question their own strongly held opinions and assumptions. Most people form their opinions on the basis of upbringing, peer pressure, and personal, cultural, or professional bias. By reading carefully balanced opposing views, readers must directly confront new ideas as well as the opinions of those with whom they disagree. This is not to simplistically argue that everyone who reads opposing views will—or should—change his or her opinion. Instead, the series enhances readers' understanding of their own views by encouraging confrontation with opposing ideas. Careful examination of others' views can lead to the readers' understanding of the logical inconsistencies in their own opinions, perspective on why they hold an opinion, and the consideration of the possibility that their opinion requires further evaluation.

Evaluating Other Opinions

To ensure that this type of examination occurs, Opposing Viewpoints books present all types of opinions. Prominent spokespeople on different sides of each issue as well as well-known professionals from many disciplines challenge the reader. An additional goal of the series is to provide a forum for other, less known, or even unpopular viewpoints. The opinion of an ordinary person who has had to make the decision to cut off life support from a terminally ill relative, for example, may be just as valuable and provide just as much insight as a medical ethicist's professional opinion. The editors have two additional purposes in including these less known views. One, the editors encourage readers to respect others' opinions—even when not enhanced by professional credibility. It is only by reading or listening to and objectively evaluating others' ideas that one can determine whether they are worthy of consideration. Two, the inclusion of such viewpoints encourages the important critical thinking skill of objectively evaluating an author's credentials and bias. This evaluation will illuminate an author's reasons for taking a particular stance on an issue and will aid in readers' evaluation of the author's ideas.

It is our hope that these books will give readers a deeper understanding of the issues debated and an appreciation of the complexity of even seemingly simple issues when good and honest people disagree. This awareness is particularly important in a democratic society such as ours in which people enter into public debate to determine the common good. Those with whom one disagrees should not be regarded as enemies but rather as people whose views deserve careful examination and may shed light on one's own.

Thomas Jefferson once said that "difference of opinion leads to inquiry, and inquiry to truth." Jefferson, a broadly educated man, argued that "if a nation expects to be ignorant and free . . . it expects what never was and never will be." As individuals and as a nation, it is imperative that we consider the opinions of others and examine them with skill and discernment. The Opposing Viewpoints Series is intended to help readers achieve this goal.

David L. Bender and Bruno Leone,
Founders

Greenhaven Press anthologies primarily consist of previously published material taken from a variety of sources, including periodicals, books, scholarly journals, newspapers, government documents, and position papers from private and public organizations. These original sources are often edited for length and to ensure their accessibility for a young adult audience. The anthology editors also change the original titles of these works in order to clearly present the main thesis of each viewpoint and to explicitly indicate the opinion presented in the viewpoint. These alterations are made in consideration of both the reading and comprehension levels of a young adult audience. Every effort is made to ensure that Greenhaven Press accurately reflects the original intent of the authors included in this anthology.

Introduction

"Our truncated public discussions of race suppress the best of who and what we are as a people because they fail to confront the complexity of the issue in a candid and critical manner."

—*Cornel West*

It is an understatement to say that race is a sensitive issue in American society. Indeed, Americans often find race relations difficult to discuss. The controversy is shaped by vociferous disagreements over the extent of discrimination in American society and how much responsibility white Americans living today have for ongoing racial inequality. Although public opinion polls indicate that a majority of Americans feel that race relations are improving, there is a significant difference in how whites and blacks perceive racial issues. For example, in a 2003 poll conducted by ABC News, 54 percent of whites polled said they thought race relations were "good" or "excellent," compared to only 44 percent of blacks. In the same poll, 80 percent of whites said that blacks have "an equal chance at jobs" compared to only 39 percent of blacks.

These differences in public opinion may reflect the fact that racial inequality is an ongoing reality in the United States. The median income for blacks in 2003 was only 62 percent of the median income for whites, and the median income for Hispanics was only 69 percent of that for whites. An estimated 22.1 percent of blacks and 21.2 percent of Hispanics lived in poverty in 2000 compared to 7.5 percent of whites. Almost 11 percent of blacks were unemployed in 2003, compared to under 7 percent of Hispanics and under 5 percent of whites. Higher rates of poverty and unemployment among minorities are linked to a variety of other racial controversies, including segregation in housing, racism in the criminal justice system, and racial disparities in health care.

Ellis Cose, a columnist and contributing editor at *Newsweek*, believes that economic inequality between blacks and whites is one of the most serious problems facing the United

States. He also claims that Americans are reluctant to talk about the problem openly, for two reasons. First, Cose maintains that "after centuries of greater or lesser racial turmoil, Americans are not terribly optimistic that the problem has a solution." Second, he says, "Discussions about race have a way of deteriorating into efforts to assign blame, and the search for villains, more often than not, ends at white America's doorstep." Cose and many other analysts maintain that discussions about race relations in America are shaped by "white guilt" over centuries of slavery and decades of legalized segregation.

To many analysts the 1960s began a period when whites accepted responsibility for centuries of discrimination against blacks. The great accomplishment of the Civil Rights Movement was that mainstream white America, along with the U.S. government, acknowledged the evils of segregation and discrimination. The Supreme Court's 1954 decision in *Brown v. Board of Education*—which made segregation in schools illegal—the Civil Rights Acts of 1957 and 1964, and the Voting Rights Act of 1965 all helped put an end to legalized segregation and discrimination and secured the guarantees of citizenship for blacks. Social welfare programs of the 1960s and afterwards, such as Lyndon Johnson's Great Society, helped reduce the economic inequalities that slavery and legalized segregation helped create. As author Cornel West writes in *Race Matters*,

> The era of the sixties was a watershed period in American history because for the first time we decided as a people to overcome the racial divide *and* declare war on poverty. . . . This was a brief moment in which we bravely confronted our most explosive issues as a people: *racial hierarchy and the maldistribution of wealth and power.*

"But," writes West, "it did not last long." Advocates for racial equality worry that the United States is experiencing a backlash against the goals West describes. Michael Brown, lead author of the book *Whitewashing Race*, is one of many observers who feel that now white Americans are rejecting the idea of "white guilt":

> Today, many white Americans are concerned only with whether they are, individually, guilty of something called

racism. Having examined their soul and concluded that they are not personally guilty of any direct act of discrimination, many whites convince themselves that they are not racists and then wash their hands of the problem posed by persistent racial inequality.

Moreover, conservative commentators are increasingly questioning the extent of racism and discrimination, and therefore the need for white guilt. In his 1995 book *The End of Racism*, Dinesh D'Souza wrote that "racism undoubtedly exists, but it no longer has the power to thwart blacks or any other group in achieving their economic, political, and social aspirations." Many black Americans, such as *Chicago Tribune* editor Don Wycliff, share this view: "Given the very real and dramatic progress African Americans have made over the last three and one-half decades, it is hard to sustain the argument that we remain, as a group, victims of unrelenting and unyielding societal racism."

Many commentators disagree with these optimistic portrayals of race relations, but even those who believe discrimination is still a serious problem now question the role that white guilt should play in improving race relations. Many writers on race, including Brown, argue that Americans must go beyond blame-oriented arguments about racism and discrimination while still acknowledging the reality of racial inequality. Much of the current economic disparity between blacks and whites, Brown argues, is not due to overt discrimination by individual whites but rather "reflects the legacy of past decisions . . . that systematically disadvantaged black Americans [and] benefited white Americans. These policies, in combination and over generations, have had enormous and pervasive consequences." In this view it is possible that race relations are improving and that individual racism has become relatively rare—but that, in economic terms, America's racial divide remains significant. Many who hold this view believe that white guilt will not prove very productive in remedying racial ills, however.

The debate over white guilt is just one of many surrounding the issue of race relations. Controversies over race relations range from the uncertainty of whether or not they are improving to questions about the effects of race-conscious policies on society. The authors in *Race Relations: Opposing Viewpoints* address these topics in the following chapters: What Is the State of Race Relations in America? Is Racism a Serious Problem? What Should the Government Do to Improve Race Relations? How Can Society Improve Race Relations? The viewpoints in this volume aim to provide readers with insights on the complexities of race relations in today's America.

CHAPTER 1

What Is the State of Race Relations in America?

Chapter Preface

Race relations, like many other controversial topics, tends to become the subject of national debate only when high-profile events bring attention to the issue. Unfortunately, in the case of race relations, the mainstream media tend to focus on racial issues only when tensions have culminated in violence.

As Ellis Cose writes in his book *Color-Blind*, "Though Americans prefer to dwell on parables of white virtue and black advancement—culminating in the flowering of good-will all around—events periodically force us to widen our gaze and to focus on terrain we would rather not see. The 1992 Los Angeles riots did that, and so did the O.J. Simpson trial." The Los Angeles riots followed the acquittal of three of the four Los Angeles Police Department officers accused in the videotaped beating of Rodney King. More than fifty people were killed, over four thousand were injured, and rioters caused approximately $1 billion in property damage. During the 1995 O.J. Simpson trial, accusations of racist conduct by the LAPD were made by the defense, and when a largely black jury acquitted Simpson of murder charges, some pundits claimed the verdict was partly in retaliation for the earlier acquittals in the Rodney King case. More recently, in April 2001, Cincinnati suffered two days of riots and looting in the wake of the killing of an unarmed black man by police.

When the media focus on race relations in the wake of tragic events such as these, the debate becomes intertwined with the specifics of each event. In contrast, the authors in the following chapter attempt to assess the more general state of America's race relations without the distortion and amplification that can accompany news reports following emotionally charged events.

"The alienation of black America is actual and ongoing."

Race Relations Are Worsening

Deborah Mathis

Deborah Mathis is a nationally syndicated columnist who has appeared on *Frontline, Inside Washington, America's Black Forum*, and many other discussion programs. The following viewpoint is excerpted from her book *Yet a Stranger: Why Black Americans Still Don't Feel at Home*. In it, she argues that black Americans face widespread dislike, disapproval, and even hatred from white Americans and that whites resent blacks for continuing to complain about prejudice. Faced with white hostility on a daily basis, she argues, many blacks are overly genial and self-effacing in their interactions with whites while other blacks try to ignore such racial tensions. Whatever strategy is adopted, however, widespread attitudinal racism has profound effects on the lives of black Americans.

As you read, consider the following questions:
1. What "one unmistakable appeal" does the "Look" make to black Americans, in the author's view?
2. What is the "fourth-grade hook," according to Mathis?
3. Why is white confusion over black agitation and protest understandable, in Mathis's opinion?

The flagrantly racist acts and policies that stain much of American history provide a certain service in that they are unambiguous. "Whites only" signs require no interpretation or discernment. However ridiculous and offensive the old-fashioned tactics and systems of racism were, they were at least straightforward. They were at least—and it pains me to apply this term to such evil, but—*honest*. It was not difficult to size up the enemy in those days.

White Resentment of Blacks

Rather than physical danger and harsh confrontation, the new common threat to the peace and prosperity of black Americans is a steady diet of indignities, disillusions, rejections, and suspicions that poison our hope, our patriotism, and our ambition. However, much of white America does not want to hear this complaint. Things are better, they declare—by every account, by any book, they have improved. They believe the 1964 Civil Rights Act, the 1965 Voting Rights Act, the proliferation of affirmative action policies, and expansive desegregation neutralized any grievances black America has about access and opportunity. Therefore, disparities that exist in income, educational attainment, and life expectancy are imaginary, greatly exaggerated, or our fault, so goes the standard spin. Believing they have ceded plenty for our sakes and in the name of equalization, doubters harbor a roiling resentment and fatigue, often encased in one famous question: What more do you people want?

The question is, of course, ludicrous and rhetorical, designed to make a statement and not solicit an answer. Those who ask it are stating, in effect, that we have overstepped our bounds, outstayed our welcome, exhausted geniality and accommodation, been overindulged and, in the process, proven ourselves to be an insatiable, greedy lot, expecting more than we have any right to ask. *What more do you people want?*

The virus of resentment and fatigue may be at large in the white community. Some of the people afflicted with it are troubled by how they've started thinking about black people and the entire equality question. Several have called me in my capacity as a newspaper columnist, seeking relief from the awful ideas that are beginning to swell in their heads. Invariably, these callers tell me that they are well educated, have enjoyed interracial friendships, have never considered themselves to be a bigot or a racist but fret that "I'm becoming one." Their reasons are usually presented with more civility and forethought than those of the occasional raging racist who writes or calls. But there is little difference in the essence of what they have to say. In either case, the argument comes down to this: Black people have as many opportunities as any other American to be healthy, safe, educated, employed, and prosperous. So, if we have babies out of wedlock, do poorly in school, end up in prison or too early in the grave, sell drugs, use crack, have dead-end jobs, and otherwise exist on life's dingy, risky, outer rim, why should white Americans have to be accountable for it, subsidize it, defer to it, apologize for it, or even worry about it? And what in the world does the long-gone institution of slavery have to do with present conditions and circumstances? After all of the loftily worded laws, the constitutional tinkering, the shared facilities, the ceded ground, the proliferation of interracial friendships and love affairs, an "Administration that looks like America"—after all this, they ask WHAT MORE DO YOU PEOPLE WANT?

The Look

More than their own exhaustion and frustration, the protestors betray a deep misunderstanding of black America and an underestimation of history's long-term effects. Except during outbreaks of vicious bigotry, it is difficult to persuade white America that the alienation of black America is actual and ongoing, afflicting each generation through policy, custom, quack sciences, and, if nothing else, the Look.

We learn to recognize the Look very early in life. It radiates from white strangers' faces. It's not the same look of benign curiosity that is cast upon the typical newcomer, but a distinct look of unease, confusion, dislike, disapproval, alarm, dread, even hatred. And it conveys myriad questions—What are you doing here? What do you want? What are you up to?—while making one unmistakable appeal: go away.

It is impossible to describe the Look to those outside its range. Sometimes, I'm sure, the transmitter is hardly aware he or she has dispatched it. But black people can feel it as sharply as the cutting wind and have learned to anticipate it, though the Look occasionally catches us off guard. If you are hit by it early in life or often enough, the Look can kill. Not your body, but your spirit. Kill your faith that you will ever belong. Kill your hopes that what you have to offer the world will ever be noticed, appreciated, nurtured, or rewarded. Kill your desire to participate, to go along, to get along. Snuff out your will to even try.

Fear of Frankness

Our country is consuming itself in racial rage. Increasingly, talk about race carries either the tone of violence or a sense of sterile, exaggerated civility. The message seems to be, Shut up and behave before somebody gets hurt. Talking about race is, quite literally, dangerous. . . .

It is hard to converse about anything while enraged. And the hold of habitual racism is harder to kick than heroin, particularly when practically everyone you know is a user and every newsstand and television set—projecting images of black violence in a ceaseless flow—is a pusher. We have reached the point where our racial hostility and stereotyping regenerate themselves, intensifying as if in an echo chamber, through the inertia of reciprocal resentment. Then, periodically, new and outrageous racial incidents provide this juggernaut with fresh momentum. Many African Americans now automatically presume that hostility from any white person, in any situation, is racially based. Many whites leap to the equivalent conclusion about blacks. Sometimes the facts bear out suspicions; sometimes they do not. But we can't see far enough past our own racial panic buttons to discern the difference.

Bruce A. Jacobs, *Race Manners: Navigating the Minefield Between Black and White Americans.* New York: Arcade, 1999.

How frequently we encounter the Look depends, in part, on where we live and do business, the cast of our skin and how much or little we reflect white norms and customs in the way we walk, talk, and dress. Blacks in the upper economic strata, especially those who dress conservatively and are well established in the American mainstream, will get the Look less often than those who are poor and less well versed in Anglo-American standards. Males who are poor and black are likely to be snared by the Look so often and harshly that the Look leaves a stab wound.

Every self-aware black American knows the Look and its cruel implications. Even those who have attempted to shed all vestiges of their blackness experience it from time to time when they arrive on unfamiliar turf before their résumés or portfolios have been introduced and they are just another black stranger to be warily surveyed.

"The Fourth-Grade Hook"

For the most part, we are spared this offense in our earliest years. As infants and toddlers, we either pass unnoticed by strangers or are treated benignly, being too young to rouse suspicion or fear. But by the time the natural rambunctiousness of youth takes hold and we begin to act and think independently, the Look begins to land on us, raising that sense of "otherness" that black people have been writing and talking about ever since Africa lost its treasure to these shores. Black educators and social workers have traced the onset of this phenomenon to about age nine. They call it "the fourth-grade hook" to mark the turning point from assumed innocent sprite to presumed developing menace. After that, the Look gradually becomes more frequent, harder and more corrosive, supplanting the presumption of innocence with the anticipation of criminality, depravity, and incompetence. It yokes the child with self-doubt, intimidation, and a definite sense of unwelcomeness, a sense of strangeness, even in his own home country. In response, the black child may become more careful and self-conscious, more cunning, or more reckless and rebellious. Whatever the response, it is a strain against the psychic chains that would bind his sense of self-worth, liberty, belonging, and happiness.

The Look is a draining thing, but there are countermeasures. One is to ignore it, to starve it of feedback. Another is to meet it with a defiant stare and rigid stance, daring the Look to turn into words or action. A third approach is to defuse the Look with broad smiles, humor, an ostentatious display of etiquette and articulation, an overdone geniality, even self-effacement—the Anti-Menace routine. We learn to command these strategies early and can conjure them reflexively. What a pitiful state of affairs it is that any American should need such a repertoire. Consider this example:

Three black teenage boys stand at a convenience store checkout counter. They are wearing the uniform of their generation: baggy pants, long T-shirts, sloppy unlaced sneakers, and, on one, a baseball cap turned backward. The clerk, a middle-aged white woman, is scowling, cutting her eye, at the teens as she serves an elderly man at the counter. When the man leaves, the first teen steps up, places a bag of chips, a soft drink, and two candy bars on the counter. He digs into his pockets for cash. The clerk snarls, "Would you wait a minute?" then mumbles something laced with disdain.

Immediately, the play unfolds. The boy widens his eyes, relaxes his jaw, and says nervously, "Oh, sorry." He scoops his goods from the counter. Behind him, his friend drops his head and gazes at the floor. The last one stares into the distance, his mouth taut, his gleamless eyes fixed and unblinking. He seems tired—sick and tired, no doubt—of a look he has seen too many times. He can't be more than sixteen years old.

Imagine that kind of reception day in, day out. In school. On the streets. At the mall. *What are you doing here? What are you up to?* Imagine being sized up and discarded on the basis of the way you walk or talk or dress or joke around. Imagine how it eats away at your joy and may eventually chew on your own goodness. Stab wounds.

The Racial Divide Is Real

At its worst, the Look threatens greater offenses—oppressive, discriminatory, and presumptuous acts, policies, practices, and laws based on assumptions. It assumes black Americans have not only a unique American experience and perspective but a distinct essence. A lesser essence. Those who don't know us believe we possess a different temperament and different natural urges, and that we lack intellectual or moral altitude, that we are by nature needy and dependent. Hence, our successes are often measured in dollars and degrees and are met with celebration and wonder as to what miracle—or what savior—intervened to lift us from our sorry original state. For many, we are still a curiosity. Even in our own country. Even at home.

White confusion over the constancy of black agitation and protest is understandable when one recognizes their unfamiliarity with the day-to-day dynamics of black life. What they see is that the first and most brazen constructs of institutional racism—slavery and segregation—have been dismantled. What even the most sensitive and sympathetic whites cannot see or know is the extent and depth of our exposure to attitudinal racism or the stubbornness of its grip or the profundity of its effects on us. The racial divide is real. It is measurable by statistical disparities in poverty, crime, scholastic achievement, health, and longevity. But it is there in the abstract too—in the lost faith and security of those who have been repeatedly scalded by the Look.

"The doors of political and economic
opportunity are wide open."

Race Relations Are Improving

Abigail Thernstrom, interviewed by Charlotte Hays

Race relations in America have improved dramatically, argues
Abigail Thernstrom in the following viewpoint. In fact, she
contends, blacks are enjoying far more upward mobility than
they did in the past. According to Thernstrom, claims that
schools, elections, and other American institutions are racially
biased are unsupported by evidence. Abigail Thernstrom is a
senior fellow at the Manhattan Institute, a member of the
Massachusetts State Board of Education, and a commissioner
on the U.S. Commission on Civil Rights. She and her husband, Harvard historian Stephan Thernstrom, are the coau-
thors of *America in Black and White: One Nation, Indivisible*.
Charlotte Hays writes for the *Women's Quarterly*.

As you read, consider the following questions:

1. According to Thernstrom, what percentage of blacks
   believe that their children will enjoy a higher standard of
   living than they do?
2. What characteristics define good schools serving the
   black community, in the author's view?
3. What charge does Thernstrom levy against the U.S.
   Commission on Civil Rights, which was involved in the
   2000 recount in Florida?

Abigail Thernstrom, interviewed by Charlotte Hays, "What Nobody Wants to
Say About Race: Author and Civil Rights Commissioner Abigail Thernstrom
Talks to Charlotte Hays," *Women's Quarterly*, Autumn 2001. Copyright © 2001
by the Independent Women's Forum, www.iwf.org. Reproduced by permission.

[*The Women's Quarterly*]: Diane McWhorter, author of *Carry Me Home, Birmingham, Alabama*, . . . had a [July 2001] piece about Birmingham in the *New York Times Magazine*. It was about the trial of the last defendant in the 1963 bombing of the Birmingham church that killed four little girls. McWhorter seemed to be saying that, despite the outward civility, little had changed in Birmingham since the bombing. What do you make of this effort to deny real progress in racial matters?

THERNSTROM: The picture has changed radically, and it is time to acknowledge that fact. McWhorter is clearly becoming one of the darlings of the moment in the mainstream media, and I have liked some of her writings in the past. But she is profoundly wrong on this question. It is time for the *New York Times* and the chattering classes in general to wake up and celebrate how far we have come. Their message to whites seems to be: It's 10:00 A.M., and it's time for your daily five minutes of guilt. The mainstream media celebrate the voices of pessimists.

The Washington Post . . . did some polling on racial attitudes and analyzed the results. In reporting on the poll, the *Post* essentially said, whites are in a state of deep denial; they don't see the radical racial inequality around them. In fact, the actual poll suggests even more confidence in the level of opportunity in American society on the part of blacks than whites. Sixty-one percent of blacks, but only 46 percent of whites, said they believed their children would enjoy a higher standard of living than they did.

TWQ: In *America in Black and White*, you and your husband [Harvard historian Stephan Thernstrom] quote the journalist Brent Staples. When Staples was in the process of being hired by the *New York Times*, he said his editor wanted to know if he was "a faux Chevy Chase [Maryland] Negro or an authentic nigger," who had grown up "poor in the ghetto, besieged by crime and violence." There is a tendency for white intellectuals to insist that blacks be hostile.

THERNSTROM: That's true, but becoming less so, which is a sign of progress. I see a dawning recognition of the diversity within the group that we call "the black community," which is not a "community," given the diversity of black experience today. There is an increasing recognition of social class differences and of differences in political values among blacks, although the divisions are not yet reflected in election results.

TWQ: In your book, you point out that there was such improvement in test scores among black children between 1980 and 1988 that, had this rate of improvement continued, African-Americans and whites would now have the same test scores. What happened?

THERNSTROM: Nobody knows what happened to stop the progress, which doesn't, in fact, matter. We don't need to know the root causes of a problem in order to try and attack it. In the case of education, we know what good schools look like. But how to put them in place across the country? That's the tough question. The entire public education system is stacked against real change.

TWQ: What do good schools look like? Often the children who most need education to better their lot in life, including blacks, get the worst schools.

THERNSTROM: Urban black students, particularly, get an education that is inadequate to their needs. Some wonderful schools are serving them very well, however. They are just few and far between. They all look more or less the same. They are highly disciplined. They offer an often-needed structure to these children's lives. They concentrate on the core subjects—reading and math, mainly. The hours are very long. The school year is very long. The teaching is superb. There is great leadership at the top of the school. And the principal is an instructional leader for all of the teachers. The students read serious literature. And they aren't allowed to wallow in victimization. The teachers deliver a very strong "no excuses" message, even though many of these kids do have a genuinely lousy life. But the teachers don't care what else is going on in their lives; they still have to learn their times tables because when they're thirty, nobody is going to ask whether life in their neighborhood was a bummer.

TWQ: What about the attack on testing as racially biased?

THERNSTROM: The tests aren't racially biased. These children need the skills that the good tests assess. These tests give us information that we need.

TWQ: As you point out in the book, many African-Americans believe that there is lingering racism and that they need the federal government to protect them. That seems to be key to a lot of what happens in politics.

The Public's Improving View of Race Relations

In a national poll conducted by ABC News and the *Washington Post* in January 2003, the number of blacks and whites who said that race relations are "good" or "excellent" rose by about 20 percentage points from a 1997 poll.

Group	2003	1997	Change
All	52%	33%	+19
Whites	54%	33%	+21
Blacks	44%	24%	+20
Others	49%	28%	+21

ABCNews.com, "Poll: Public Believes Race Relations Are Getting Better," January 23, 2003.

THERNSTROM: There are good historical reasons why blacks feel so vulnerable without the protective arm of the federal government. It was, after all, the federal government that really broke the back of the Jim Crow South. Federal courts intervened with judicial decisions that insisted upon racial equality. Federal legislation changed the status of blacks almost overnight. But the era of dependence on the federal government should be over. And today, many government regulations are, in fact, impediments to black progress. Government is the problem, not the solution. For instance, the regulatory maze in a city like Chicago is an obstacle course for inexperienced would-be entrepreneurs, many of whom are black and Hispanic. The Institute for Justice has long been attacking this problem; it has been representing blacks and Hispanics whose private sector dreams are thwarted by public sector rules.

TWQ: The African-American vote is essential to the Democratic Party. Neither [Jimmy] Carter nor [Bill] Clinton would have been president without it. I sometimes wonder if some of the bitterness that is injected into politics is just a form of demagoguery, an effort to hold onto this group of voters.

THERNSTROM: Sure, but the Democrats don't have a monopoly when it comes to demagoguery which is endemic in politics. Such demagoguery, however, is particularly destructive on the issue of race. The Democratic Party keeps ratcheting up the sense, on the part of blacks, that they are victims, that the deck is stacked against them. And thus we have a racially defined group in America whose members feel angry and alienated—who feel that this country is not their country. And that's a danger to the fragile fabric of American politics and society.

TWQ: Let's talk about the U.S. Civil Rights Commission on which you now serve. Tell me about its involvement in the recount in Florida [during the 2000 presidential election], and the hearings that were held and your role in the hearings.

THERNSTROM: The commission held three days of hearings in Florida. And it heard countless witnesses. The bottom line for me: The election was far from perfect in Florida, which was undoubtedly true in other states as well. But, race per se, racial discrimination per se, played absolutely no part in the outcome. And that, of course, runs counter to the commission's report. Its central finding was that blacks were nine times more likely than whites—and I'm putting it in a passive voice deliberately because the commission's report puts it in a passive voice—to find that their ballots had been spoiled. The implication was that somehow [Florida governor] Jeb Bush and [former Florida secretary of state] Katherine Harris figured out which ballots were cast by black voters and managed to crumple them up. Or mutilate them in some way. . . .

TWQ: Was there any real evidence that blacks were prevented from voting in Florida?

THERNSTROM: No. There was some evidence that some poll workers were not very helpful to any voters (regardless of race or ethnicity), and there were stories of confusion and jammed phone lines. Perhaps most compelling of all was the evidence of insufficient accommodations for the disabled. But none of these problems had anything to do with race. In fact, there was a witness in Florida who said she had problems with poll workers. I said to her, "Look, it sounds to me as if you had difficulties at the polls, which you shouldn't have had. But it doesn't look to me as if it had anything to do with race." And she said, "Race? Who was talking about race? These were black poll workers." So yes, there were problems. And the state of Florida has taken steps to remedy them. Was there anything distinctive about the problems in that state? I don't think so, but nobody else has put any other state under a microscope, either now or in previous elections. . . .

TWQ: I am going to ask a cynical question. As I said, African-Americans are an important constituency to the Democratic Party. Could the commission's report on Florida's voting be pure demagoguery?

THERNSTROM: Absolutely. . . . The majority on the commission were determined to paint George W. Bush as an illegitimate president. And that's what the Florida report was all about. And they clearly wanted to send a message to black voters that Bush is not their president and that the Republican Party is not their party. It's a dangerous message. The commission seems determined to reinforce the belief on the part of too many blacks that they are a separate nation within our nation, outsiders to the American experiment. In fact, precisely the opposite message should be delivered. Blacks are Americans whose families have been here for well over 200 years. They have shaped American culture in a myriad of important and wonderful ways. And the doors of political and economic opportunity are wide open.

"The American political and economic system enables a diverse society to coexist in harmony most of the time."

Americans Are Embracing Diversity

Dominic J. Pulera

Dominic J. Pulera is the author of *Visible Differences: Why Race Will Matter to Americans in the Twenty-First Century*, from which the following viewpoint is excerpted. He discusses the predictions made by demographers that by 2050 whites will not be the dominant racial group in the United States. Pulera rejects the idea that increased immigration and greater ethnic diversity will fragment the nation. He acknowledges that, given the opportunity, many Americans do choose to move to racially homogenous areas. But he also notes that the most heavily populated areas in the United States are increasingly heterogeneous, and he argues that people in these areas are adapting well to diversity.

As you read, consider the following questions:

1. In what year did *Time* run its cover story predicting a "white-minority America," according to Pulera?
2. What name does the author use to describe Americans born after 1982?
3. What effect does the author believe the events of September 11, 2001, had on race relations in America?

Multiculturalism affects the lives of an increasing number of Americans . . . , because every year the United States becomes a little more ethnically and racially diverse than it was during the previous 12 months. In . . . much of America, this phenomenon is largely attributable to minority birth rates that exceed those of the white population. But immigration and, to a lesser extent, domestic in-migration contribute as much as the birth rates to the ethnic and racial heterogeneity found in such places as Texas, Illinois, California, and New York. More than a decade ago demographers began to consider seriously the possibility that the United States would lose its white majority someday. *Time* did its part with a sensational 1990 story about the end of white-majority America, a demographic milestone the newsmagazine projected would occur sometime during the 2050s. Emblazoned across *Time's* cover was a watercolor rendering of the American flag, with the title "America's Changing Colors," and the open-ended question: "What will the U.S. be like when whites no longer are the majority?"

The White-Minority-America Argument

The white-minority-America argument consists of a simple syllogism:

   a. The United States is becoming proportionally less white each year.
   b. This ineluctable development will transform almost every sector of American society. It is, of course, a desirable process because diversity itself is an intrinsic good.
   c. Therefore, we should begin preparing for a white-minority America immediately, through affirmative action and other manifestations of multiculturalism, so the transition to the nonwhite-majority America of the future goes smoothly and seamlessly.

Since that cover story in *Time* . . . , "the coming white minority," as Dale Maharidge describes it, has been accepted as an article of faith—largely without debate. At the very least, America may turn into a *white-plurality* country, because whites will not be a minority so much as a plurality of the population. By 2050 the U.S. Census (middle series) projections forecast that America will be 52.8% white, 24.5% Hispanic, 13.6% black, 8.2% Asian, and 0.9% American Indian. Indeed, a more heterogeneous white-majority America, not a white-minority America, seems to be the most likely scenario at this point.

The white-plurality-America scenario presupposes trans-minority group interests—the idea that all racial minorities will form a cohesive majority united in opposition to the white minority in almost every situation. This is a specious argument: People of color frequently ally with whites against each other. Hispanics now rival blacks as the nation's largest minority group, a quantum shift with myriad consequences and ramifications that have yet to be felt. As Americans learn more about race and ethnicity, and events continue to unfold in our largest cities, it is becoming ever-more difficult to predict how well blacks and Latinos will get along with each other. Asian Americans, particularly those who are middle-class suburbanites, tend to align closely with their white neighbors on most issues. Many factors . . . add an element of uncertainty to the process of forecasting America's racial demographics 50 years from now. . . .

The Millennials

In the interregnum, younger Americans are most likely to be comfortable with the twenty-first century's multiracial environment. Neil Howe and William Strauss describe the generation "born in or after 1982" as "the Millennials." They have had greater exposure to multicultural curricula, in addition to nonwhite playmates and cultural heroes, than most persons aged 50 and older. Despite periodic instances of skinhead violence and widely publicized reports of racial fights in high schools, American youths are increasingly comfortable with mixed groups of teens dating, fraternizing, working together, and attending school with each other. But they lack firsthand familiarity with the traumatic events of the 1960s, which inspired many Baby Boomers' sappy assumptions about racial integration and social justice 30 years ago.

The Millennials are the first generation of American youths to grow up with multiracial sensibilities. As Howe and Strauss point out, "Millennials have never personally seen black-white race issues divide America." Their pop cultural experiences included the likes of Brandy and Chris Rock, Jennifer Lopez and Carlos Santana, Lucy Liu and Jackie Chan. Yet some evidence suggests that these multicultural pioneers may accept benign notions of social segregation. Young adults emphatically agree on the need for equal opportunities for people of all races, but they do not necessarily feel that everyone has to hang out together all the time in integrated social settings.

Less and Less Privilege Associated with Being White

For all their sins throughout history, one has to give white Americans credit for learning from experience. . . . Like it or not, it's impossible for them to escape the impacts of a browned commercial culture. White men are the very template for the Borg of *Star Trek* fame; they will adapt to what they cannot assimilate by force. As whiteness continues to lose its overall premium in commercial culture, more and more whites are forced to take stock of their investment in whiteness. Most of this examination is taking place in academic and intellectual circles and barely touches the average white person over, say, thirty-five. But other adaptations are taking place in under-thirty-five America. One of the most telling is the rising rate of interracial marriage, up some tenfold since 1960, with most of the increase coming since 1980. To be sure, in 1980 just 5 percent of whites were married to someone of another race or of Hispanic origin. But more striking than the marriage numbers (which will take several more decades to move deep into the double digits) are the figures on attitudes. Somewhere in the early 1990s the proportion of white Americans who approve of mixed black and white marriages crossed into the majority. In 1997 it was 61 percent. The factors behind this trend of course are varied and complex, but I don't think they can be positively correlated with growing political liberalism or social sensitivity. Rather, I think they owe more to a kind of desensitization that comes from the declining premium on whiteness and the declining discount on nonwhiteness in commercial popular culture.

Leon E. Wynter, *American Skin: Pop Culture, Big Business, and the End of White America*. New York: Random House, 2002.

Every day Americans cast votes in what might be described as the never-ending, national referendum on racial reconciliation. Frequently, we cast affirmative ballots by giving persons of other races the benefit of the doubt on the road, at the mall, and in the workplace. Less frequently, we cast negative ballots by uttering racial epithets, giving dirty looks, rejecting job applications, or not renting properties to qualified buyers. Xenophobes frequently utter the infelicitous phrase, "Go back to (the presumed native country of the person in question)," when they come into contact with immigrants who irritate them. Sometimes nativists instigate their own informal Americanization efforts by crudely exhorting immigrants to speak English, when they hear the unfamiliar sounds of Korean, Spanish, or some other foreign tongue.

All the while, personal, interpersonal, and institutional efforts to reconcile racial differences continue. . . .

Migration Patterns and Diversity

Domestic migration patterns are [an] indicator of American racial attitudes. Whole swaths of America harbor unwitting trendsetters in the field of domestic migration patterns: native-born white and, to a far lesser extent, black migrants who have fled heterogeneous metropolitan areas, due to high concentrations of nonwhite immigrants. "Push" factors driving the new regional segregation center around immigration and assorted ephemera related to it, like competition for jobs and feelings of cultural dislocation. "Pull" factors motivating domestic migrants depend on the people and their end destinations, but may include climate, a lower cost of living, a booming job market, and a corporate-friendly environment. Race, to be sure, is not necessarily the paramount concern of the typical domestic migrant, but issues related to racial and ethnic diversity usually influence his or her decision to move to a more homogeneous area of the country.

Domestic migrants often desert cities and suburbs in the racially heterogeneous states and take refuge in the racially homogeneous parts of the Mountain West and Pacific Northwest. They flee the conspicuously multicultural environments of such places as California and New York, and often go to places with negligible populations of recent immigrants. Between 1990 and 2000 the Los Angeles-Riverside-Orange County metropolitan area shed 843,000 whites. Similarly, metropolitan New York lost 680,000 whites. There is evidence, too, that suggests African Americans have been fleeing urban neighborhoods that are now dominated by Latinos. The tremendous population growth attributable to immigrants and their offspring masks the departures of native-born whites and blacks from the Californias and New Yorks. So even though the census figures for aggregate population appear virtually unchanged for the ten-year period from 1990 to 2000, the racial demographics of many metropolitan areas underwent sweeping changes during those years.

Racial Diversity Is Becoming the Norm

In the end, the consequences of this developing demographic polarization will depend on how durable a phenomenon it proves to be. Perhaps the most significant ramifications affect the young people, the ones who are going to be the cultural, business, and political leaders of tomorrow. Many of them—white and nonwhite—will hail from areas where significant ethnic and racial diversity is the norm. While the days are long gone when a white youth might not see blacks or Asian Americans in person until he went into the Army, or went away to school, clearly some Caucasian youths will have far more exposure to America's multicultural splendor than others. And while it is clear that familiarity with such matters—and the ability to acknowledge, manage, and respect diversity—will be absolutely necessary for almost any job description, at least nationally, it is not so clear that growing up in a multiracial environment gives one special insights in this regard. Most public school teachers, moreover, use curricular materials that familiarize their students with America's heterogeneous demographics.

Increasing racial diversity, much of it fueled by immigration, is changing the faces of countless American communities and inspiring discussions about how to integrate the newcomers without acrimony. Dozens of American towns and cities have diversity committees, whose members discuss the local demographics, formulate plans to promote inclusion and assimilation, and remain vigilant for signs of racial polarization in their communities. Sometimes these committees take shape in the aftermath of a catalytic event that exposes the divisions in a given place. Other times, the committees are organized by people of good faith who wish to prevent schisms and divisions from developing in their communities.

Numerous American towns and cities have been changed immeasurably by immigration during the past few decades and have not had any major problems in integrating the new-comers. Wausau, Wisconsin, a primarily white community in the north-central part of the Badger State, is now home to a sizable Hmong population. A giant pork-processing plant has reshaped the demographics of Guymon, Oklahoma, a white-majority town in the Oklahoma Panhandle where Hispanics now account for 38.4% of the population. White immigrants from Turkey and Arabia prosper in Paterson, New Jersey, a predominantly black and Latino city that contains one of the nation's most comprehensive Middle Eastern shopping districts. To be sure, many parts of America still remain largely untouched by the effects of ethnic and racial heterogeneity. These places are sparsely populated and usually rural.

Unity Out of Diversity

In any event, America certainly is more united than the skeptics thought, as we saw in the aftermath of the terrorist attacks on the World Trade Center and the Pentagon on September 11, 2001. Almost immediately, there was a widespread outpouring of national support and unity. Americans came together faster than at any other time since World War II, crossing ethnic, racial, religious, and socioeconomic lines to do so. There were nationalistic, pro-American messages everywhere, from billboards to storefronts to automobiles, with such slogans as "United We Stand" and "In God We Trust." Americans of all races watched the patriotic television specials. We used the "United We Stand" postage stamps. The ubiquitous American flags popped up immediately after the attacks, and they waved from black, Hispanic, Asian-American, and American Indian homes and vehicles just as readily as they did from white residences and automobiles.

After all, the terrorists did not make ethnic, racial, religious, and socioeconomic distinctions in their war on America: Every American was a potential target. This realization undoubtedly contributed to the American public's nearly unanimous support for the war against the Taliban and Al Qaeda in Afghanistan.[1] Many Americans contributed money to the relief efforts that aided the families who lost loved ones in the terrorist attacks; as of February 2002, $1.5 billion had been raised for this purpose. It remains to be seen how lasting this new sense of national unity will be, but it definitely is a hopeful sign that Americans are far more united than we had all thought before the terrorist attacks.

Even the treatment of Arab Americans and Muslim Americans in the aftermath of September 11 testified, at least to some extent, to the unity, tolerance, and goodwill of the American people. As is typically the case when the United States becomes involved in a Middle Eastern conflict, there was a sharp uptick in the amount of harassment directed against Arab Americans, Muslim Americans, and individuals who were mistaken for members of these two groups. By February 2002, the Council on American-Islamic Relations had collected in excess of 1,700 instances of bias in the five months since September 2001. These manifestations of the nativist impulse included hate mail, ethnic slurs, public harassment, employment discrimination, and school confrontations. After the September 11 attacks, however, many Americans, from President [George W.] Bush and his surrogates to millions of ordinary people, consistently made it clear in their words and deeds that Arab Americans and American Muslims were vital members of the American family, not enemies of America.

Cautious Optimism

Therefore, most of us do not lose sleep at night worrying that twenty-first-century America will be a multiethnic dystopia, where one's particularistic loyalties are solely to his or her ethno-racial group. A 1995 *Newsweek* survey found that, in response to the question, "100 years from today, will the United States still exist as one nation?" 61% of whites, 54% of Hispanics, and only 41% of blacks polled answered

---

1. In the fall of 2001, the United States invaded Afghanistan to oust the ruling Taliban, which was harboring members of the al Qaeda terrorist group. Al Qaeda has been fingered for carrying out the September 11 attacks.

affirmatively. Their cautious optimism is justified: The American political and economic system enables a diverse society to coexist in harmony most of the time. The economic expansion of the 1990s may have healed some of the ethnic and racial tensions that still bedevil parts of our country, by ameliorating some of the conditions that underlie social maladies and festering resentments.

Looking toward the future, even if whites lose their majority status, they are not going to suffer a corresponding diminution in their economic and political power—that is, if white-plurality states California and New Mexico, and multiethnic cities such as Chicago and Los Angeles, are any indication. In such situations, power sharing usually takes place; whether it is tokenism or meaningful depends on the circumstances. Indeed, the future stability of the United States may depend on the willingness of socially dominant groups to share power with racial and ethnic minorities. These efforts aimed at integration and reconciliation will affect every one of us in some way during the twenty-first century.

"Block by block and institution by institution [the United States] is a relatively homogeneous nation."

Most Americans Have Not Embraced Diversity

David Brooks

David Brooks is a contributing editor of *Newsweek*, a senior editor of the *Weekly Standard*, and a political analyst for the *NewsHour with Jim Lehrer.* In the following viewpoint he argues that despite mainstream rhetoric about the value of diversity, most Americans prefer to associate with people who are like themselves. Brooks writes that this tendency is most evident in matters of race and ethnicity: Despite decades of government efforts to end housing discrimination and encourage integration, evidence suggests that there remains a clear tendency for neighborhoods to become more racially homogeneous over time. Brooks concludes that diversity is an ideal that Americans celebrate in the abstract but do not uphold in their daily lives.

As you read, consider the following questions:
1. In Brooks's view, why do new neighborhoods tend to start out integrated, then become more racially and ethnically homogeneous over time?
2. In what ways are elite universities very homogeneous, in the author's opinion?
3. What does Brooks suggest would be a good means of bringing more diversity to young people's lives?

Maybe it's time to admit the obvious. We don't really care about diversity all that much in America, even though we talk about it a great deal. Maybe somewhere in this country there is a truly diverse neighborhood in which a black Pentecostal minister lives next to a white anti-globalization activist, who lives next to an Asian short-order cook, who lives next to a professional golfer, who lives next to a postmodern-literature professor and a cardiovascular surgeon. But I have never been to or heard of that neighborhood. Instead, what I have seen all around the country is people making strenuous efforts to group themselves with people who are basically like themselves.

Human beings are capable of drawing amazingly subtle social distinctions and then shaping their lives around them. In the Washington, D.C., area Democratic lawyers tend to live in suburban Maryland, and Republican lawyers tend to live in suburban Virginia. If you asked a Democratic lawyer to move from her $750,000 house in Bethesda, Maryland, to a $750,000 house in Great Falls, Virginia, she'd look at you as if you had just asked her to buy a pickup truck with a gun rack and to shove chewing tobacco in her kid's mouth. In Manhattan the owner of a $3 million SoHo loft would feel out of place moving into a $3 million Fifth Avenue apartment. A West Hollywood interior decorator would feel dislocated if you asked him to move to Orange County. In Georgia a barista from Athens would probably not fit in serving coffee in Americus.

It is a common complaint that every place is starting to look the same. But in the information age, the late writer James Chapin once told me, every place becomes more like itself. People are less often tied down to factories and mills, and they can search for places to live on the basis of cultural affinity. Once they find a town in which people share their values, they flock there, and reinforce whatever was distinctive about the town in the first place. Once Boulder, Colorado, became known as congenial to politically progressive mountain bikers, half the politically progressive mountain bikers in the country (it seems) moved there; they made the place so culturally pure that it has become practically a parody of itself.

Happiness from Homogeneity

But people love it. Make no mistake—we are increasing our happiness by segmenting off so rigorously. We are finding places where we are comfortable and where we feel we can flourish. But the choices we make toward that end lead to the very opposite of diversity. The United States might be a diverse nation when considered as a whole, but block by block and institution by institution it is a relatively homogeneous nation.

When we use the word "diversity" today we usually mean racial integration. But even here our good intentions seem to have run into the brick wall of human nature. Over the past generation reformers have tried heroically, and in many cases successfully, to end housing discrimination. But recent patterns aren't encouraging: according to an analysis of the 2000 census data, the 1990s saw only a slight increase in the racial integration of neighborhoods in the United States. The number of middle-class and upper-middle-class African-American families is rising, but for whatever reasons—racism, psychological comfort—these families tend to congregate in predominantly black neighborhoods.

In fact, evidence suggests that some neighborhoods become more segregated over time. New suburbs in Arizona and Nevada, for example, start out reasonably well integrated. These neighborhoods don't yet have reputations, so people choose their houses for other, mostly economic reasons. But as neighborhoods age, they develop personalities (that's where the Asians live, and that's where the Hispanics live), and segmentation occurs. It could be that in a few years the new suburbs in the Southwest will be nearly as segregated as the established ones in the Northeast and the Midwest.

Predictable Clusters

Even though race and ethnicity run deep in American society, we should in theory be able to find areas that are at least culturally diverse. But here, too, people show few signs of being truly interested in building diverse communities. If you run a retail company and you're thinking of opening new stores, you can choose among dozens of consulting firms that are quite effective at locating your potential customers. They can do this because people with similar tastes and preferences tend to congregate by ZIP code.

The most famous of these precision marketing firms is Claritas, which breaks down the U.S. population into sixty-two psycho-demographic clusters, based on such factors as how much money people make, what they like to read and watch, and what products they have bought in the past. For example, the "suburban sprawl" cluster is composed of young families making about $41,000 a year and living in fast-growing places such as Burnsville, Minnesota, and Bensalem, Pennsylvania. These people are almost twice as likely as other Americans to have three-way calling. They are two and a half times as likely to buy Light n' Lively Kid Yogurt. Members of the "towns & gowns" cluster are recent college graduates in places such as Berkeley, California, and Gainesville, Florida. They are big consumers of DoveBars and *Saturday Night Live*. They tend to drive small foreign cars and to read *Rolling Stone* and *Scientific American*.

Looking through the market research, one can sometimes be amazed by how efficiently people cluster—and by how predictable we all are. If you wanted to sell imported wine, obviously you would have to find places where rich people live. But did you know that the sixteen counties with the greatest proportion of imported-wine drinkers are all in the same three metropolitan areas (New York, San Francisco, and Washington, D.C.)? If you tried to open a motor-home dealership in Montgomery County, Pennsylvania, you'd probably go broke, because people in this ring of the Philadelphia suburbs think RVs are kind of uncool. But if you traveled just a short way north, to Monroe County, Pennsylvania, you would find yourself in the fifth motor-home-friendliest county in America.

Geography is not the only way we find ourselves divided from people unlike us. Some of us watch Fox News, while others listen to NPR. Some like David Letterman, and others—typically in less urban neighborhoods—like Jay Leno. Some go to charismatic churches; some go to mainstream churches. Americans tend more and more often to marry people with education levels similar to their own, and to befriend people with backgrounds similar to their own.

The Persistence of Racial Segregation in Housing

If one asks a representative sample of white Americans today whether people should be able to live wherever they want to regardless of race, 99% will answer "yes." Very few whites now openly subscribe to principles of racial inequality.

If, however, one asks the same sample of white Americans if they would be willing to vote for a community law that made it illegal to discriminate on the basis of race, only a minority answer "yes." And if one asks them how they feel about being around African Americans, one finds that they are damn uncomfortable. According to the latest polling data, around 25% of white Americans would object if a family member brought a black person home for dinner and a sizeable majority express discomfort at the thought of living in a neighborhood that was one-third black. Although whites may have rejected racism in principle, they remain deeply torn and uncomfortable about its implications and practice. . . .

Social scientists have referred to this "new racism" using a variety of labels: ambivalent racism, laissez faire racism, symbolic racism, modern racism, aversive racism. Whatever one calls it, the characteristic form of racism today is the acceptance of open markets in principle, but a reluctance to use government power to ensure race neutrality in practice and residual discomfort at the obvious corollary of a race blind society: extensive social interactions with African Americans on a regular and equal-status basis.

These attitudes are both a cause and a consequence of the persistence of residential segregation between blacks and whites in American society.

Douglas Massey, *Black Renaissance/Renaissance Noir*, Spring 2003.

My favorite illustration of this latter pattern comes from the first, noncontroversial chapter of *The Bell Curve*. Think of your twelve closest friends, Richard J. Herrnstein and Charles Murray write. If you had chosen them randomly from the American population, the odds that half of your twelve closest friends would be college graduates would be six in a thousand. The odds that half of the twelve would have advanced degrees would be less than one in a million. Have any of your twelve closest friends graduated from Harvard, Stanford, Yale, Princeton, Caltech, MIT, Duke, Dartmouth, Cornell, Columbia, Chicago, or Brown? If you chose your friends randomly from the American population, the odds against your having four or more friends from those schools would be more than a billion to one.

Many of us live in absurdly unlikely groupings, because we have organized our lives that way.

Diversity in Higher Education

It's striking that the institutions that talk the most about diversity often practice it the least. For example, no group of people sings the diversity anthem more frequently and fervently than administrators at just such elite universities. But elite universities are amazingly undiverse in their values, politics, and mores. Professors in particular are drawn from a rather narrow segment of the population. If faculties reflected the general population, 32 percent of professors would be registered Democrats and 31 percent would be registered Republicans. Forty percent would be evangelical Christians. But a recent study of several universities by the conservative Center for the Study of Popular Culture and the American Enterprise Institute found that roughly 90 percent of those professors in the arts and sciences who had registered with a political party had registered Democratic. Fifty-seven professors at Brown were found on the voter-registration rolls. Of those, fifty-four were Democrats. Of the forty-two professors in the English, history, sociology, and political-science departments, all were Democrats. The results at Harvard, Penn State, Maryland, and the University of California at Santa Barbara were similar to the results at Brown.

What we are looking at here is human nature. People want to be around others who are roughly like themselves. That's called community. It probably would be psychologically difficult for most Brown professors to share an office with someone who was pro-life, a member of the National Rifle Association, or an evangelical Christian. It's likely that hiring committees would subtly—even unconsciously—screen out any such people they encountered. Republicans and evangelical Christians have sensed that they are not welcome at places like Brown, so they don't even consider working there. In fact, any registered Republican who contemplates a career in academia these days is both a hero and a fool. So, in a semi-self-selective pattern, brainy people with generally liberal social mores flow to academia, and brainy people with generally conservative mores flow elsewhere.

Ideals vs. Reality

The dream of diversity is like the dream of equality. Both are based on ideals we celebrate even as we undermine them daily. (How many times have you seen someone renounce a high-paying job or pull his child from an elite college on the grounds that these things are bad for equality?) On the one hand, the situation is appalling. It is appalling that Americans know so little about one another. It is appalling that many of us are so narrow-minded that we can't tolerate a few people with ideas significantly different from our own. It's appalling that evangelical Christians are practically absent from entire professions, such as academia, the media, and filmmaking. It's appalling that people should be content to cut themselves off from everyone unlike themselves.

The segmentation of society means that often we don't even have arguments across the political divide. Within their little validating communities, liberals and conservatives circulate half-truths about the supposed awfulness of the other side. These distortions are believed because it feels good to believe them.

On the other hand, there are limits to how diverse any community can or should be. I've come to think that it is not useful to try to hammer diversity into every neighborhood and institution in the United States. Sure, Augusta National should probably admit women, and university sociology departments should probably hire a conservative or two. It would be nice if all neighborhoods had a good mixture of ethnicities. But human nature being what it is, most places and institutions are going to remain culturally homogeneous.

It's probably better to think about diverse lives, not diverse institutions. Human beings, if they are to live well, will have to move through a series of institutions and environments, which may be individually homogeneous but, taken together, will offer diverse experiences. It might also be a good idea to make national service a rite of passage for young people in this country: it would take them out of their narrow neighborhood segment and thrust them in with people unlike themselves. Finally, it's probably important for adults to get out of their own familiar circles. If you live in a coastal, socially liberal neighborhood, maybe you should take out a subscription to *The Door*, the evangelical humor magazine; or maybe you should visit Branson, Missouri. Maybe you should stop in at a megachurch. Sure, it would be superficial familiarity, but it beats the iron curtains that now separate the nation's various cultural zones.

Look around at your daily life. Are you really in touch with the broad diversity of American life? Do you care?

"Two great, immutable forces have driven America's attitudes . . . around race. The first has been white racism, and the second has been white guilt."

White Guilt over Racial Issues Contributes to Poor Race Relations

Shelby Steele

Shelby Steele is a research fellow at the Hoover Institution at Stanford University and the author of *A Dream Deferred: The Second Betrayal of Black Freedom in America.* In the following viewpoint he argues that Americans have become too quick to blame racism for the problems facing black Americans. Steele believes that instead white guilt and black victimhood are to blame. He contends that today white guilt causes many Americans and institutions to view blacks largely in terms of their skin color. In turn, black youths view themselves primarily as part of an oppressed group. He concludes that this emphasis on racial identities is undermining real progress in race relations.

As you read, consider the following questions:

1. Why does Steele view the black college student he describes as a figure of pathos?
2. Under the stigma of white guilt, according to Steele, what must American institutions perpetually prove?
3. What is the sole purpose of black group identity, in the author's view?

Shelby Steele, "The Age of White Guilt: The Disappearance of the Black Individual," *Harper's Magazine*, vol. 305, November 2002, p. 33. Copyright © 2002 by *Harper's Magazine*. All rights reserved. Reproduced by permission.

Not long ago C-SPAN carried a Harvard debate on affirmative action between conservative reformer Ward Connerly and liberal law professor Christopher Edley. During the Q and A a black undergraduate rose from a snickering clump of black students to challenge Mr. Connerly, who had argued that the time for racial preferences was past. Once standing, this young man smiled unctuously, as if victory were so assured that he must already offer consolation. But his own pose seemed to distract him, and soon he was sinking into incoherence. There was impatience in the room, but it was suppressed. Black students play a role in campus debates like this and they are indulged.

The campus forum of racial confrontation is a ritual that has changed since the sixties in only one way. Whereas blacks and whites confronted one another back then, now black liberals and black conservatives do the confronting while whites look on—relieved, I'm sure—from the bleachers. I used to feel empathy for students like this young man, because they reminded me of myself at that age. Now I see them as figures of pathos. More than thirty years have passed since I did that sort of challenging, and even then it was a waste of time. Today it is perseveration to the point of tragedy.

Black Victimhood

Here is a brief litany of obvious truths that have been resisted in the public discourse of black America over the last thirty years: a group is no stronger than its individuals; when individuals transform themselves they transform the group; the freer the individual, the stronger the group; social responsibility begins in individual responsibility. Add to this an indisputable fact that has also been unmentionable: that American greatness has a lot to do with a culturally ingrained individualism, with the respect and freedom historically granted individuals to pursue their happiness—this despite many egregious lapses and an outright commitment to the oppression of black individuals for centuries. And there is one last obvious but unassimilated fact: ethnic groups that have asked a lot from their individuals have done exceptionally well in America even while enduring discrimination.

Now consider what this Harvard student is called upon by

his racial identity to argue in the year 2002. All that is creative and imaginative in him must be rallied to argue the essential weakness of his own people. Only their weakness justifies the racial preferences they receive decades after any trace of anti-black racism in college admissions. The young man must not show faith in the power of his people to overcome against any odds; he must show faith in their inability to overcome without help. As Mr. Connerly points to far less racism and far more freedom and opportunity for blacks, the young man must find a way, against all the mounting facts, to argue that black Americans simply cannot compete without preferences. If his own forebears seized freedom in a long and arduous struggle for civil rights, he must argue that his own generation is unable to compete on paper-and-pencil standardized tests.

It doesn't help that he locates the cause of black weakness in things like "structural racism" and "uneven playing fields," because there has been so little correlation between the remedies for such problems and actual black improvement. Blacks from families that make $100,000 a year or more perform worse on the SAT than whites from families that make $10,000 a year or less. After decades of racial preferences blacks remain the lowest performing student group in American higher education. And once they are out of college and in professions, their own children also underperform in relation to their white and Asian peers. Thus, this young man must also nurture the idea of a black psychological woundedness that is baroque in its capacity to stifle black aspiration. And all his faith, his proud belief, must be in the truth of this woundedness and the injustice that caused it, because this is his only avenue to racial pride. He is a figure of pathos because his faith in racial victimization is his only release from racial shame.

Group Racial Identity vs. the Individual

Right after the sixties' civil-rights victories came what I believe to be the greatest miscalculation in black American history. Others had oppressed us, but this was to be the first "fall" to come by our own hand. We allowed ourselves to see a greater power in America's liability for our oppression than we saw in ourselves. Thus, we were faithless with ourselves just when we had given ourselves reason to have such faith. We couldn't have made a worse mistake. We have not been the same since.

To go after America's liability we had to locate real transformative power outside ourselves. Worse, we had to see our fate as contingent on America's paying off that liability. We have been a contingent people ever since, arguing our weakness and white racism in order to ignite the engine of white liability. And this has mired us in a protest-group identity that mistrusts individualism because free individuals might jeopardize the group's effort to activate this liability.

Today I would be encouraged to squeeze my little childhood experience of individuality into a narrow group framework that would not endanger the group's bid for white intervention. I would be urged to embrace a pattern of reform that represses our best hope for advancement—our individuals—simply to keep whites "on the hook."

Mr. Connerly was outnumbered and outgunned at that Harvard debate. The consensus finally was that preferences would be necessary for a while longer. Whites would remain "on the hook." The black student prevailed, but it was a victory against himself. In all that his identity required him to believe, there was no place for him. . . .

The Age of White Guilt

Two great, immutable forces have driven America's attitudes, customs, and public policies around race. The first has been white racism, and the second has been white guilt. The civil-rights movement was the dividing line between the two. Certainly there was some guilt before this movement, and no doubt some racism remains after it. But the great achievement of the civil-rights movement was that its relentless moral witness finally defeated the legitimacy of racism as propriety—a principle of social organization, manners, and customs that defines decency itself. An idea controls culture when it achieves the invisibility of propriety. And it must be remembered that racism was a propriety, a form of decency. When, as a boy, I was prohibited from entering the fine Christian home of the occasional white playmate, it was to save the household an indecency. Today, thanks to the civil-rights movement, white guilt is propriety—an utterly invisible code that defines decency in our culture with thousands of little protocols we no longer even think about. We have been living in an age of white guilt for four decades now.

A Contest to Establish or Escape Guilt

Our whole racial "dialogue" has become a contest to establish or escape guilt, and, as a result, is shot through with dishonesty.

Most white people—or what appears to me to be most—seem intent mainly on establishing their personal innocence: innocence of racial bias, of discrimination, of any connection to or benefit from slavery. Not only is this beside the point, it's also impossible. One cannot escape the personal implications of membership in a society, no matter how personally blameless one may be. Where race in America is concerned, there are no innocents.

For their part, black people—or at least black leaders—seem more intent than ever on pressing the issue of white personal guilt: for slavery, for segregation, for lingering discrimination, for whatever deficits African Americans still suffer. More than three decades into the nation's effort to pay off that promissory note Martin Luther King Jr. spoke of in his "I Have a Dream" speech, black leaders seem intent on denying that anything at all has changed, determined not to "let the white man off the hook.". . . . The notion of acting as moral prosecutor and judge of a fellow human being strikes me as odious.

Don Wycliff, *Commonweal*, June 1, 2001.

What is white guilt? It is not a personal sense of remorse over past wrongs. White guilt is literally a vacuum of moral authority in matters of race, equality, and opportunity that comes from the association of mere white skin with America's historical racism. It is the stigmatization of whites and, more importantly, American institutions with the sin of racism. Under this stigma white individuals and American institutions must perpetually prove a negative—that they are not racist—to gain enough authority to function in matters of race, equality, and opportunity. If they fail to prove the negative, they will be seen as racists. Political correctness, diversity policies, and multiculturalism are forms of deference that give whites and institutions a way to prove the negative and win reprieve from the racist stigma.

Institutions especially must be proactive in all this. They must engineer a demonstrable racial innocence to garner enough authority for simple legitimacy in the American democracy. No university today, private or public, could admit students by academic merit alone if that meant no black or brown faces on campus. Such a university would be seen as racist and shunned accordingly. White guilt has made social engineering for black and brown representation a condition of legitimacy.

People often deny white guilt by pointing to its irrationality—"I never owned a slave," "My family got here eighty years after slavery was over." But of course almost nothing having to do with race is rational. That whites are now stigmatized by their race is not poetic justice; it is simply another echo of racism's power to contaminate by mere association.

The other common denial of white guilt has to do with motive: "I don't support affirmative action because I'm guilty; I support it because I want to do what's fair." But the first test of sincere support is a demand that the policy be studied for effectiveness. Affirmative action went almost completely unexamined for thirty years and has only recently been briefly studied in a highly politicized manner now that it is under threat. The fact is that affirmative action has been a very effective racial policy in garnering moral authority and legitimacy for institutions, and it is now institutions—not individual whites or blacks—that are fighting to keep it alive.

The real difference between my parents and myself was that they protested in an age of white racism and I protested in an age of white guilt. They were punished; I was rewarded. By my time, moral authority around race had become a great and consuming labor for America. Everything from social programs to the law, from the color of TV sitcom characters to the content of school curricula, from college admissions to profiling for terrorists—every aspect of our culture—now must show itself redeemed of the old national sin. Today you cannot credibly run for president without an iconography of white guilt: the backdrop of black children, the Spanish-language phrases, the word "compassion" to separate conservatism from its associations with racism.

Collecting the Fruits of White Guilt

So then here you are, a black American living amidst all this. Every institution you engage—the government, universities, corporations, public and private schools, philanthropies, churches—faces you out of a deficit of moral authority. Your race is needed everywhere. How could you avoid the aggressions, and even the bigotries, of white guilt? What institution could you walk into without having your color tallied up as a credit to the institution? For that matter, what political party or ideological direction could you pursue without your race being plundered by that party or ideology for moral authority?

Because blacks live amidst such hunger for the moral authority of their race, we embraced protest as a permanent identity in order to capture the fruits of white guilt on an ongoing basis. Again, this was our first fall by our own hand. Still, it is hard to imagine any group of individuals coming out of four centuries of oppression and not angling their identity toward whatever advantage seemed available. White guilt held out the promise of a preferential life in recompense for past injustice, and the protest identity seemed the best way to keep that promise alive.

An obvious problem here is that we blacks fell into a group identity that has absolutely no other purpose than to collect the fruits of white guilt. And so the themes of protest—a sense of grievance and victimization—evolved into a sensibility, an attitude toward the larger world that enabled us always and easily to feel the grievance whether it was there or not. Protest became the mask of identity, because it defined us in a way that kept whites "on the hook." Today the angry rap singer and Jesse Jackson and the black-studies professor are all joined by an unexamined devotion to white guilt.

To be black in my father's generation, when racism was rampant, was to be a man who was very often victimized by racism. To be black in the age of white guilt is to be a victim who is very rarely victimized by racism. Today in black life there is what might be called "identity grievance"—a certainty of racial grievance that is entirely disconnected from actual grievance. And the fervor of this symbiosis with white guilt has all but killed off the idea of the individual as a source of group strength in black life. All is group and unity, even as those minority groups that ask much of their individuals thrive in America despite any discrimination they encounter. . . .

Recognizing Individuals Rather than Races

[Black American writer] James Baldwin once wrote: "What Europe still gives an American is the sanction, if one can accept it, to become oneself." If America now gives this sanction to most citizens, its institutions still fiercely deny it to blacks. And this society will never sanction blacks in this way until it drops all the mechanisms by which it tries to appease white guilt. Guilt can be a very civilizing force, but only when it is simply carried as a kind of knowledge. Efforts to appease or dispel it will only engage the society in new patterns of dehumanization against the same people who inspired guilt in the first place. This will always be true.

Restraint should be the watchword in racial matters. We should help people who need help. There are, in fact, no races that need help; only individuals, citizens. Over time maybe nothing in the society, not even white guilt, will reach out and play on my race, bind me to it for opportunity. I won't ever find in America what Baldwin found in Europe, but someday maybe others will.

"No genuine dialogue about race is possible when millions of whites are taught to believe that . . . the 'race problem' has now been solved."

White Denial of Racial Issues Contributes to Poor Race Relations

Manning Marable

Manning Marable is a professor of history and political science, and director of the Institute for Research in African-American Studies, at Columbia University. The following viewpoint is excerpted from his book *The Great Walls of Democracy: The Meaning of Race in American Life*. In it, he rejects the idea that America should de-emphasize or "move beyond" racial issues in its efforts to become a "color-blind" society. In his view these suggestions are made by whites who want to believe that racial inequality is a thing of the past and that America does not owe anything to blacks. On the contrary, Marable writes, discrimination and inequality cannot be overcome by pretending they do not exist. Marable also rejects the idea that blacks should surrender their own unique culture and history in order to view themselves as part of the broader American whole.

As you read, consider the following questions:

1. What two movies does Marable cite to explain his view that whites deny the importance of racial issues?
2. What incident did the media publicize as an example of "black bigotry," in the author's view?

In post–civil rights era America, most white commentators on issues of race emphasize the necessity for all of us to become "color blind." That is, we should be "blind" to any imputed differences that tend to divide people by skin color or phenotype, by physical appearance, or by genetic background. The political version of this argument is that any special measures that created privileged classes based on racial categories are inherently unfair and discriminatory.

Forgive and Forget?

The color-blind thesis almost always is accompanied by an appeal to "forgive and forget." The logic of this argument goes as follows: Black Americans were certainly terribly oppressed during slavery and Jim Crow segregation. But no white Americans alive today owned slaves. There's been much social progress in recent years, thanks to the constructive cooperation between the races. It's time for us to move beyond ancient grievances and racial bitterness, toward taking greater personal responsibility for our own lives. All of us bear part of the blame for the burden of prejudice—that is, the minorities themselves are partly responsible for getting themselves into their current predicament.

With certain variations, this basic argument is repeated over and over again in the white media by white political leaders and institutions about the dynamics of race. Their thesis is that African Americans must stop being so "sensitive" and "defensive" about the problems of their people and communities. Whites have nothing to apologize for, and African Americans have little really to complain about.

In popular films and culture, the message is largely the same. At the beginning of *Die Hard with a Vengeance* (1995), a white actor, Bruce Willis, stands in Harlem, just off Amsterdam Avenue, wearing a huge sign that reads: "I Hate Niggers." A cluster of justifiably outraged young black men surrounds the undercover white cop. Yet the film, remarkably, portrays not the white cop, but the African-American males, as emotional, dangerous, unstable, and threatening. In the award-winning film *Pulp Fiction* (1994), a white criminal played by John Travolta "accidentally" blows off the head of a young black man when his gun discharges. Covered with blood and gore, the white killer and his black partner (Samuel L. Jackson) take refuge in the suburban home of a white criminal associate (Quentin Tarantino). The suburban mobster is outraged that this "dead nigger" has been dragged into his home. Yet to display that he could not really be a racist, the film then cuts away to show that this bigot is married to an African-American woman. The fact that he has a sexual relationship with a black woman is supposed to clear up any misunderstandings about his repeated stream of utterances about "dead niggers"!

Blaming Blacks for Racial Tension

The white corporate-oriented media loves to publicize stories about "black bigotry." Several years ago, for instance, when the Oakland, California, board of education suggested that African-American young people may learn best in an environment that validates the language they actually speak ("ebonics") in their neighborhoods and in daily interactions with friends, blacks everywhere were attacked for "rejecting" standard English, as if none of us speak it. When African-American students now demand black studies courses, or advocate campus housing emphasizing Caribbean, African, and black American cultural traditions and identity, they are subjected to ridicule as proponents of "self-segregation."

We will never uproot racism by pretending that everyone shares an equal and common responsibility for society's patterns of discrimination and inequality. Black people were never "equal partners" in the construction of slavery, Jim Crow segregation, and ghettoization. We weren't individually or collectively consulted when our criminal-justice system imprisoned one-third of our young men, or when we continue to be burdened with twice the unemployment rate of whites. To be "color blind" in a virulently racist society is to be blind to the history and reality of oppression. To forget the past and to refuse to acknowledge the color-coded hierarchies that constitute our parallel racial universes is to evade any responsibility for racial peace in the future.

Celebrate Black History

Perhaps the greatest lie in the arsenal of the "color-blind" proponents of racism is the assertion that black people can be understood only as part of the larger narrative of standard American history. That is to say that "black history" is somehow inferior to or at odds with "American history." To be part of the national project, culturally and ideologically, means that we must surrender and abandon those lessons we've learned in our struggles along the way.

While it is certainly true that black Americans are survivors of a very destructive historical process from slavery, Jim Crow segregation, and ghettoization, we know within ourselves that we have never stood silently by, succumbing to the forces of white oppression. Any understanding of black history illustrates that we have consistently fought to maintain a unique set of cultural values that have shaped and continue to define our core identities as a people. We have, in effect, always been not only the makers of "our" history but also central to the construction and evolution of the larger American experience.

Celebrate Black Culture

What are the cultural reservoirs that create the psychological, emotional, and cultural foundation of the strength and vision that the adventure of blackness in American life has produced? Even in the shadows of slavery, we found our humanity in the gift of song. Our music tells us much about who we are, how we have worked, how we have loved, where we've been, and where we're going. From the blues of the Mississippi Delta, to the soaring sounds of bebop in Harlem in the 1940s, to the provocative rhythms of today's hip hop, black music reflects the pulse and sensibility of blackness.

Black history and culture reveal the gift of grace, the fluidity of motion and beauty that an oppressed people have claimed as their own. It is constantly recreated in many ways: from the artistry of dance to the spectacular athleticism of Michael Jordan. Grace is the ability to redefine the boundaries of possibility. We as a people were not supposed to survive the ordeal of oppression and Jim Crow segregation, yet our very existence speaks to the creative power of our collective imagination. That power is reflected in our language, the rhythm of gospel, and the power of black preachers on Sunday morning in our churches. That power is found in the creative energy of our poets and playwrights. The gift of grace can be heard in the writings of Toni Morrison, James Baldwin, Amiri Baraka, and Alice Walker.

Attitudes in Black and White

In a national poll conducted by ABC News and the *Washington Post* in January 2003, a much higher percentage of whites than blacks felt that racism was not a problem in their community.

Think blacks in your community have:	Whites	Blacks	Gap
An equal chance at jobs	80%	39%	41
Equal treatment from police	66	28	38
Equal treatment from merchants	82	45	37
An equal chance in housing	81	46	35
Equal chance at good public schools	92	58	34

ABCNews.com, "Poll: Public Believes Race Relations Are Getting Better," January 23, 2003.

The experience of work has always been the foundation of black strength and capacity-building throughout history. Slavery was the only moment in American history when people of African descent experienced full employment: Everybody worked. If financial gain was commensurate with hard work, African Americans would undoubtedly be among the wealthiest people on earth. Yet despite our economic marginalization, despite the historic pattern of receiving barely 60 cents for every dollar of wages that comparable white work commands, we nevertheless have found real meaning in the world of work. Black labor, more than any other, is responsible for establishing much of the foundations of the economic productivity of this country. Black working-class women and men have for generations been at the forefront of the trade-union movement and collective efforts to improve the quality of life and the conditions of work for all Americans.

And then there is the historical strength of family and community, kinship and neighbors within the black experience. An oppressed people cannot survive unless there is close cooperation and mutual support by and for each other.

The reservoir of strength within the black family has been anchored in our recognition that kinship is collective, not nuclear, in structure.

Throughout black history, along with the strength of family there has been the strength of our faith. During slavery, a prayer was in many ways an act of resistance. When we sang "Steal Away to Jesus," our eyes looked to the North Star, to the faraway promised land of freedom. Today that faith still resounds as the cultural heart of black community life in thousands of towns and cities across the country. From the courage of Dr. Martin Luther King, Jr., to the contemporary activism of a Jesse Jackson or an Al Sharpton, black faith has been most powerful as a historical force when spirituality reinforces fundamental social change.

Whites Must Acknowledge Blacks' Unique History

It is only through the telling of our stories about the destructive dynamics of racialization that many white Americans will be able finally to come to terms with the social costs of "whiteness," for themselves, their children, and for the larger society. No genuine dialogue about race is possible when millions of whites are taught to believe that blacks have been marginal to the construction of American society, or that the "race problem" has now been solved.

No meaningful dialogue can take place when some whites still think about race as a "zero-sum game," where any economic or political advances by racial minorities come at their expense. I believe that the only way for us to move toward a nonracist society is for white Americans to acknowledge that the struggles and sacrifices that blacks have made to destroy structural racism in all of its forms throughout history have directly contributed to enriching and expanding the meaning of democracy not just for ourselves, but for everyone within our society.

> *"The* reconquista *(re-conquest) of the Southwest United States by Mexican immigrants is well underway."*

Hispanic Immigration Threatens to Divide America

Samuel P. Huntington

Samuel P. Huntington is chairman of the Harvard Academy for International and Area Studies and the author of *Who Are We?: The Challenges to America's National Identity*, from which the following viewpoint is adapted. Huntington argues that Hispanic immigration into the U.S. Southwest threatens to divide the United States into two peoples with different cultures and languages. Huntington lists a variety of ways in which Hispanic immigrants are different from most other immigrants. For example, he notes that because the United States and Mexico share a common border, it is easier for Mexican immigrants to maintain ties to their home country. For these and other reasons, Huntington warns that a predominantly Hispanic culture is emerging in the Southwest, one that will be in many respects separate from the rest of the United States.

As you read, consider the following questions:
1. What are the six factors that make Mexican immigration unique, in Huntington's view?
2. What percent of total legal immigration did Mexicans account for in the 1990s, according to the author?
3. According to F. Chris Garcia, what is the one thing that every Hispanic wants to protect and promote?

Samuel P. Huntington, *Who Are We?: The Challenges to America's National Identity*. New York: Simon & Schuster, Inc., 2004. Copyright © 2004 by Samuel P. Huntington. Reproduced by permission of Simon & Schuster Macmillan.

The single most immediate and most serious challenge to America's traditional identity comes from the immense and continuing immigration from Latin America, especially from Mexico, and the fertility rates of these immigrants compared to black and white American natives. Americans like to boast of their past success in assimilating millions of immigrants into their society, culture, and politics. But Americans have tended to generalize about immigrants without distinguishing among them and have focused on the economic costs and benefits of immigration, ignoring its social and cultural consequences. As a result, they have overlooked the unique characteristics and problems posed by contemporary Hispanic immigration. The extent and nature of this immigration differ fundamentally from those of previous immigration, and the assimilation successes of the past are unlikely to be duplicated with the contemporary flood of immigrants from Latin America. This reality poses a fundamental question: Will the United States remain a country with a single national language and a core Anglo-Protestant culture? By ignoring this question, Americans acquiesce to their eventual transformation into two peoples with two cultures (Anglo and Hispanic) and two languages (English and Spanish). . . .

A World of Difference

Contemporary Mexican and, more broadly, Latin American immigration is without precedent in U.S. history. The experience and lessons of past immigration have little relevance to understanding its dynamics and consequences. Mexican immigration differs from past immigration and most other contemporary immigration due to a combination of six factors: contiguity, scale, illegality, regional concentration, persistence, and historical presence.

Contiguity. Americans' idea of immigration is often symbolized by the Statue of Liberty, Ellis Island, and, more recently perhaps, New York's John F. Kennedy Airport. In other words, immigrants arrive in the United States after crossing several thousand miles of ocean. U.S. attitudes toward immigrants and U.S. immigration policies are shaped by such images. These assumptions and policies, however, have little or no relevance for Mexican immigration. The United States is now confronted by a massive influx of people from a poor, contiguous country with more than one third the population of the United States. They come across a 2,000-mile border historically marked simply by a line in the ground and a shallow river.

This situation is unique for the United States and the world. No other First World country has such an extensive land frontier with a Third World country. The significance of the long Mexican-U.S. border is enhanced by the economic differences between the two countries. "The income gap between the United States and Mexico," Stanford University historian David Kennedy has pointed out, "is the largest between any two contiguous countries in the world." Contiguity enables Mexican immigrants to remain in intimate contact with their families, friends, and home localities in Mexico as no other immigrants have been able to do.

Scale. The causes of Mexican, as well as other, immigration are found in the demographic, economic, and political dynamics of the sending country and the economic, political, and social attractions of the United States. Contiguity, however, obviously encourages immigration. Mexican immigration increased steadily after 1965. About 640,000 Mexicans legally migrated to the United States in the 1970s; 1,656,000 in the 1980s; and 2,249,000 in the 1990s. In those three decades, Mexicans accounted for 14 percent, 23 percent, and 25 percent of total legal immigration. These percentages do not equal the rates of immigrants who came from Ireland between 1820 and 1860, or from Germany in the 1850s and 1860s. Yet they are high compared to the highly dispersed sources of immigrants before World War I, and compared to other contemporary immigrants. To them one must also add the huge numbers of Mexicans who each year enter the United States illegally. Since the 1960s, the numbers of foreign-born people in the United States have expanded immensely, with Asians and Latin Americans replacing Europeans and Canadians, and diversity of source dramatically giving way to the dominance of one source: Mexico. Mexican immigrants constituted 27.6 percent of the total foreign-born U.S. population in 2000. The next largest contingents,

Chinese and Filipinos, amounted to only 4.9 percent and 4.3 percent of the foreign-born population.

From Diversity to Dominance
Foreign-Born Population Living in the United States

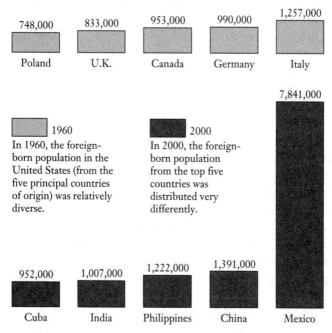

Samuel P. Huntington, "The Hispanic Challenge," *Foreign Policy*, March/April 2004.

In the 1990s, Mexicans composed more than half of the new Latin American immigrants to the United States and, by 2000, Hispanics totaled about one half of all migrants entering the continental United States. Hispanics composed 12 percent of the total U.S. population in 2000. This group increased by almost 10 percent from 2000 to 2002 and has now become larger than blacks. It is estimated Hispanics may constitute up to 25 percent of the U.S. population by 2050. These changes are driven not just by immigration but also by fertility. In 2002, fertility rates in the United States were estimated at 1.8 for non-Hispanic whites, 2.1 for blacks, and 3.0 for Hispanics. "This is the characteristic shape of developing countries," the *Economist* commented in 2002. "As the bulge of Latinos enters peak child-bearing age in a decade or two, the Latino share of America's population will soar."

In the mid–19th century, English speakers from the British Isles dominated immigration into the United States. The pre-World War I immigration was highly diversified linguistically, including many speakers of Italian, Polish, Russian, Yiddish, English, German, Swedish, and other languages. But now, for the first time in U.S. history, half of those entering the United States speak a single non-English language.

Illegality. Illegal entry into the United States is over-whelmingly a post-1965 and Mexican phenomenon. For almost a century after the adoption of the U.S. Constitution, no national laws restricted or prohibited immigration, and only a few states imposed modest limits. During the following 90 years, illegal immigration was minimal and easily controlled. The 1965 immigration law, the increased availability of transportation, and the intensified forces promoting Mexican emigration drastically changed this situation. Apprehensions by the U.S. Border Patrol rose from 1.6 million in the 1960s to 8.3 million in the 1970s, 11.9 million in the 1980s, and 14.7 million in the 1990s. Estimates of the Mexicans who successfully enter illegally each year range from 105,000 (according to a binational Mexican-American commission) to 350,000 during the 1990s (according to the U.S. Immigration and Naturalization Service). . . .

The United States' Quebec?

Regional Concentration. The U.S. Founding Fathers considered the dispersion of immigrants essential to their assimilation. That has been the pattern historically and continues to be the pattern for most contemporary non-Hispanic immigrants. Hispanics, however, have tended to concentrate regionally: Mexicans in Southern California, Cubans in Miami, Dominicans and Puerto Ricans (the last of whom are not technically immigrants) in New York. The more concentrated immigrants become, the slower and less complete is their assimilation. . . .

Persistence. Previous waves of immigrants eventually subsided, the proportions coming from individual countries fluctuated greatly, and, after 1924, immigration was reduced to a trickle. In contrast, the current wave shows no sign of ebbing and the conditions creating the large Mexican component of that wave are likely to endure, absent a major war or recession. . . .

Historical Presence. No other immigrant group in U.S. history has asserted or could assert a historical claim to U.S. territory. Mexicans and Mexican Americans can and do make that claim. Almost all of Texas, New Mexico, Arizona, California, Nevada, and Utah was part of Mexico until Mexico lost them as a result of the Texan War of Independence in 1835–1836 and the Mexican-American War of 1846–1848. Mexico is the only country that the United States has invaded, occupied its capital—placing the Marines in the "halls of Montezuma"—and then annexed half its territory. Mexicans do not forget these events. Quite understandably, they feel that they have special rights in these territories. "Unlike other immigrants," Boston College political scientist Peter Skerry notes, "Mexicans arrive here from a neighboring nation that has suffered military defeat at the hands of the United States; and they settle predominantly in a region that was once part of their homeland. . . . Mexican Americans enjoy a sense of being on their own turf that is not shared by other immigrants."

At times, scholars have suggested that the Southwest could become the United States' Quebec. Both regions include Catholic people and were conquered by Anglo-Protestant peoples, but otherwise they have little in common. Quebec is 3,000 miles from France, and each year several hundred thousand Frenchmen do not attempt to enter Quebec legally or illegally. History shows that serious potential for conflict exists when people in one country begin referring to territory in a neighboring country in proprietary terms and to assert special rights and claims to that territory. . . .

Spanish as a Second Language

The size, persistence, and concentration of Hispanic immigration tends to perpetuate the use of Spanish through successive generations. The evidence on English acquisition and Spanish retention among immigrants is limited and ambiguous. In 2000, however, more than 28 million people in the United States spoke Spanish at home (10.5 percent of all people over age five), and almost 13.8 million of these spoke English worse than "very well," a 66 percent increase since 1990. According to a U.S. Census Bureau report, in 1990 about 95 percent of Mexican-born immigrants spoke Spanish at home; 73.6 percent of these did not speak English very well; and 43 percent of the Mexican foreign-born were "linguistically isolated." An earlier study in Los Angeles found different results for the U.S.-born second generation. Just 11.6 percent spoke only Spanish or more Spanish than English, 25.6 percent spoke both languages equally, 32.7 percent more English than Spanish, and 30.1 percent only English. In the same study, more than 90 percent of the U.S.-born people of Mexican origin spoke English fluently. Nonetheless, in 1999, some 753,505 presumably second-generation students in Southern California schools who spoke Spanish at home were not proficient in English.

English language use and fluency for first- and second-generation Mexicans thus seem to follow the pattern common to past immigrants. Two questions remain, however. First, have changes occurred over time in the acquisition of English and the retention of Spanish by second-generation Mexican immigrants? One might suppose that, with the rapid expansion of the Mexican immigrant community, people of Mexican origin would have less incentive to become fluent in and to use English in 2000 than they had in 1970. Second, will the third generation follow the classic pattern with fluency in English and little or no knowledge of Spanish, or will it retain the second generation's fluency in both languages? Second-generation immigrants often look down on and reject their ancestral language and are embarrassed by their parents' inability to communicate in English. Presumably, whether second-generation Mexicans share this attitude will help shape the extent to which the third generation retains any knowledge of Spanish. If the second generation does not reject Spanish outright, the third generation is also likely to be bilingual, and fluency in both languages is likely to become institutionalized in the Mexican-American community.

Spanish retention is also bolstered by the overwhelming

majorities (between 66 percent and 85 percent) of Mexican immigrants and Hispanics who emphasize the need for their children to be fluent in Spanish. These attitudes contrast with those of other immigrant groups. The New Jersey-based Educational Testing Service finds "a cultural difference between the Asian and Hispanic parents with respect to having their children maintain their native language." In part, this difference undoubtedly stems from the size of Hispanic communities, which creates incentives for fluency in the ancestral language. Although second- and third-generation Mexican Americans and other Hispanics acquire competence in English, they also appear to deviate from the usual pattern by maintaining their competence in Spanish. Second- or third-generation Mexican Americans who were brought up speaking only English have learned Spanish as adults and are encouraging their children to become fluent in it. Spanish-language competence, University of New Mexico professor F. Chris Garcia has stated, is "the one thing every Hispanic takes pride in, wants to protect and promote.". . .

Blood Is Thicker than Borders

Massive Hispanic immigration affects the United States in two significant ways: Important portions of the country become predominantly Hispanic in language and culture, and the nation as a whole becomes bilingual and bicultural. The most important area where Hispanization is proceeding rapidly is, of course, the Southwest. As historian Kennedy argues, Mexican Americans in the Southwest will soon have "sufficient coherence and critical mass in a defined region so that, if they choose, they can preserve their distinctive culture indefinitely. They could also eventually undertake to do what no previous immigrant group could have dreamed of doing: challenge the existing cultural, political, legal, commercial, and educational systems to change fundamentally not only the language but also the very institutions in which they do business."

Anecdotal evidence of such challenges abounds. In 1994, Mexican Americans vigorously demonstrated against California's Proposition 187—which limited welfare benefits to children of illegal immigrants—by marching through the streets of Los Angeles waving scores of Mexican flags and carrying U.S. flags upside down. In 1998, at a Mexico–United States soccer match in Los Angeles, Mexican Americans booed the U.S. national anthem and assaulted U.S. players. Such dramatic rejections of the United States and assertions of Mexican identity are not limited to an extremist minority in the Mexican-American community. Many Mexican immigrants and their offspring simply do not appear to identify primarily with the United States.

Empirical evidence confirms such appearances. A 1992 study of children of immigrants in Southern California and South Florida posed the following question: "How do you identify, that is, what do you call yourself?" None of the children born in Mexico answered "American," compared with 1.9 percent to 9.3 percent of those born elsewhere in Latin America or the Caribbean. The largest percentage of Mexican-born children (41.2 percent) identified themselves as "Hispanic," and the second largest (36.2 percent) chose "Mexican." Among Mexican-American children born in the United States, less than 4 percent responded "American," compared to 28.5 percent to 50 percent of those born in the United States with parents from elsewhere in Latin America. Whether born in Mexico or in the United States, Mexican children overwhelmingly did not choose "American" as their primary identification.

Demographically, socially, and culturally, the *reconquista* (reconquest) of the Southwest United States by Mexican immigrants is well underway. A meaningful move to reunite these territories with Mexico seems unlikely, but Prof. Charles Truxillo of the University of New Mexico predicts that by 2080 the southwestern states of the United States and the northern states of Mexico will form *La Republica del Norte* (The Republic of the North). Various writers have referred to the southwestern United States plus northern Mexico as "Mex-America" or "Amexica" or "Mexifornia." "We are all Mexicans in this valley," a former county commissioner of El Paso, Texas, declared in 2001.

This trend could consolidate the Mexican-dominant areas of the United States into an autonomous, culturally and linguistically distinct, and economically self-reliant bloc within the United States. "We may be building toward the one thing that will choke the melting pot," warns former National Intelligence Council Vice Chairman Graham Fuller, "an ethnic area and grouping so concentrated that it will not wish, or need, to undergo assimilation into the mainstream of American multi-ethnic English-speaking life.". . .

Continuation of this large immigration (without improved assimilation) could divide the United States into a country of two languages and two cultures. A few stable, prosperous democracies—such as Canada and Belgium—fit this pattern. The differences in culture within these countries, however, do not approximate those between the United States and Mexico, and even in these countries language differences persist. Not many Anglo-Canadians are equally fluent in English and French, and the Canadian government has had to impose penalties to get its top civil servants to achieve dual fluency. Much the same lack of dual competence is true of Walloons and Flemings in Belgium. The transformation of the United States into a country like these would not necessarily be the end of the world; it would, however, be the end of the America we have known for more than three centuries. Americans should not let that change happen unless they are convinced that this new nation would be a better one.

*"A predominantly Hispanic Texas is less
likely to reflect the fears of social theorists
. . . and more likely to resemble present-
day San Antonio—messy and complex."*

Hispanic Immigration Does Not Threaten to Divide America

Jan Jarboe Russell

Jan Jarboe Russell is a journalist and the coauthor of *San Antonio: A Cultural Tapestry*. In the following viewpoint she takes issue with a 2004 article by Samuel Huntington in which the historian argues that Hispanic immigrants in the American Southwest resist assimilating into U.S. culture. Russell contrasts Huntington's portrayals with the Texas town of Sonterra. She describes the Mexican immigrants living in Sonterra as well-to-do, English-speaking, and eager to pursue the American dream. Russell argues that the Anglo and Hispanic cultures of Sonterra intermingle and borrow from one another. In her view, rather than resisting assimilation, Mexican immigrants are embracing—and contributing to—the melting pot of American culture.

As you read, consider the following questions:

1. By the third generation, what percent of Mexican-Americans speak primarily English, according to Russell?
2. What three terms does Henry Munoz III use to describe the future of Texas?

Jan Jarboe Russell, "Viva la Diferencia," *Texas Monthly*, vol. 32, June 2004, p. 68.

"My clients from Mexico are very sophisticated," said realtor Connie Ramirez as she wheeled her four-door gray Mercedes to the front gate of Sonterra, a plush gated community thirteen miles north of downtown San Antonio that is known as Monterrey North because so many rich citizens from Mexico own homes there. "They like new, large houses with verandas for entertaining that remind them of Cancun. In Mexico these people live like royalty. They want a country club lifestyle in San Antonio. That's why they like Sonterra." The security guard smiled and waved Ramirez through the gate. That day the pretty, auburn-haired Ramirez had six families from Mexico in town shopping for houses. The console of her car was crowded with maps, pens, and notepads, tools that she uses to keep track of her deals in progress. Every time her silver cell phone rang, she clamped it to her ear and called out brightly, "¡Hola!" One of her clients, a soap opera producer from Mexico City, called to check in. He had a house for sale for $560,000 in a section of Sonterra called the Highlands. That week there had been two offers—both for $530,000—but he had refused both. "I don't think he really wants to leave San Antonio," Ramirez said. As she drove through the streets of Sonterra, which are lined with young live oak trees and earth-toned stucco homes with tile roofs, Ramirez described the development's appeal to wealthy Mexicans. "I would say the number one reason my clients from Mexico love it here is security," said Ramirez. "In Mexico these people live in fear of kidnapping or assassination. They all have bodyguards. Some of the wives tell me that they can't even walk around their own homes without guards following them around. Here they don't have to worry about any of that. They can leave the bodyguards at home."

Indeed, Sonterra has been designed to ease their anxiety. Each section has its own gate, equipped with guards and video cameras. Private security guards patrol the streets in white cars marked "Security/Securitas." Once inside, freedom rules. Young, ponytailed wives drive their Jaguars and BMWs to the country club to play tennis or golf. Nannies supervise toddlers on Sonterra's crowded playground. "There goes the son of one of my clients," Ramirez said, pointing to a twenty-something speeding around a corner on a street called Las Aguas in a black Lexus SUV. "In Mexico, it would be risky for him to drive on his own like that—without a bodyguard—to the movies or to go shopping. Here, he's free."

Racial Division?

When most Texans think of the state's coming Hispanic majority, they don't, as a rule, picture the worldly, discerning inhabitants of Sonterra. Instead, they picture roiling waves of poor Hispanics who will sap their education and social-service systems and contribute little to the prosperity and prestige of the state. They see a Texas divided into two cultures—one white, one brown; one Anglo, one Hispanic, with separate languages and loyalties. The most controversial article on this subject to date, titled "The Hispanic Challenge," appeared in the March–April (2004) issue of *Foreign Policy*; it was written by Harvard professor Samuel Huntington, the author of the well-regarded *Clash of Civilizations and the Remaking of World Order*. Huntington argues that Hispanic, and particularly Mexican, immigrants are not assimilating into America's melting pot the way other nationalities and ethnic groups have in the past. Instead of coming from a different continent—like the Irish, the Germans, and the Jews of the nineteenth century—the immigrants from Mexico are coming from a contiguous territory, into areas that once belonged to their forebears. Huntington is especially concerned that because these immigrants are coming in such large numbers, they don't have to give up their language and culture. "If this trend continues, the cultural division between Hispanics and Anglos could replace the racial division between blacks and whites as the most serious cleavage in U.S. society," Huntington wrote.

Viewed through his eyes, the future of Texas is conflicted, a long-running Battle of the Alamo between Anglos and a permanent underclass of Hispanic immigrants. The numbers are frightening in that regard: Steve Murdock the state's demographer, says that by 2030, more than 50 percent of the population of Texas will be Hispanic. But in Huntington's fear-soaked analysis—he bemoans the fact that in 1998

"Jose" replaced "Michael" as the most popular name for newborn boys in California and Texas—he forgets that a shared border creates common interests as well as conflicts. San Antonio, for instance, is already 58 percent Mexican American and reveals a very different future from the one Huntington describes, one that is both more complicated and more hopeful.

Pursuing the American Dream

Meet Alfonso Tomita, for instance, a Mexican citizen who owns a thriving restaurant called Sushi/Zushi just outside the front gates of Sonterra. It was the pursuit of the American dream that first brought him to San Antonio, in 1995. He and his wife, Cristina, were both born in Mexico City. Alfonso's parents immigrated to Mexico from Japan. "Like many people in Mexico, I always had the dream of living the American way," said Alfonso, who is a living rebuttal to Huntington's characterization of Mexican immigrants as poor, uneducated, and unwilling to assimilate. He speaks English. He has a master's of business in finance from the University of Texas at San Antonio. He has investors from both Mexico and the United States. He and Cristina also moved to San Antonio because his three children—ages thirteen, eleven, and nine—suffered from respiratory problems due to the pollution in Mexico City. "And for the same reason that anyone comes to America—to build a better life for my kids," he said.

The Tomitas now own three sushi restaurants in San Antonio. Last year they grossed $1 million. Their menu offers traditional Japanese sushi, but the chefs—most of them Mexican immigrants—also make a San Antonio roll, with sprouts and crabmeat in a tangy salsa. Alfonso picked sushi because his eldest son thought it was trendy and had observed that San Antonio already had plenty of Mexican restaurants. "In most sushi restaurants, if you don't look Asian, you stay in the back kitchen, out of sight," said Alfonso. "But I totally empower the Mexican chefs. I put them right in front, making sushi in front of the customers." The check at his restaurant comes with three ways to say "thank you"—"arigato," "gracias," and "thank you." The future that Alfonso is building is not Anglo or Hispanic: Its multicultural and based on the desire for prosperity. He plans to open a Sushi/Zushi in Austin. . . .

"The Culture Is Intermingled"

Huntington argues that Mexicans who come to the United States are creating a parallel society, a Mexico within the United States. "As their numbers increase, [Hispanics] become more committed to their own ethnic identity and culture," he says. The truth is that Huntington paints a limited picture of Mexican immigration and the culture it creates; in the Southwest in particular, the Anglo and Hispanic cultures have long been sampling from each other. "We Mexicans come here, you Americans go there," said Jose Oleszcovski, a developer in Queretaro, a colonial city due north of Mexico City. "The people go back and forth, the money goes back and forth, the culture is intermingled. It's been that way for centuries."

Problems with the French Quebec–Hispanic Southwest Analogy

An analogy between Quebec and the hypothetical Mexican American separatist movement does not hold up. The French Canadians of Quebec have not simply been pro-French language, but anti-English. But while Mexican American leaders have sometimes raised the preservation of language as a rallying cry for ethnic mobilization, they have not done so in opposition to the acquisition of English. Mexico lost more than half of its national territory to the United States after the Texas insurrection and the Mexican War, but Mexican Americans have no historic memory comparable to the French Canadian memory of the loss that followed the defeat of French armies by the British on the Plains of Abraham in 1763. In Quebec, the Catholic Church nursed that grievance and promoted French separatism. In contrast, the Church in the American Southwest called for the integration of Mexican immigrants and their descendants through instruction and preparation for citizenship, classes in English, and youth activities such as those promoted by the Catholic Youth Organization.

Lawrence H. Fuchs, *American Prospect*, August 2004.

At 45, Oleszcovski is a stocky man who wears handmade shirts and designer glasses on his weekend trips to San Antonio. He travels in his own private plane. His air of authority and hurried demeanor is Donald Trump–like. In Queretaro, he oversees multiple businesses, including an industrial park that he built with Houston developer Gerald Hines. "In Mexico I work fifteen hours a day, and then I go home to a large house with many employees," said Oleszcovski. "I bought two town houses in Sonterra because I wanted a place to relax." He and his second wife live in one; the other is a guest house sometimes occupied by his grown children from his first marriage. Instead of recreating his harried Mexican life here, Oleszcovski has chosen a simpler existence. His town house is two stories and simply furnished with contemporary furniture—leather couches and chairs, glass tables—and several Rufino Tamayo paintings on the wall. His terrace overlooks Sonterra's tennis courts. "I like to read here," he said, pointing to a thick stack of books and articles. "I'm too busy to read in Mexico." This is a man who has reversed existing cultural stereotypes. In Mexico, he lives the stressful life of a captain of industry. In San Antonio, he succumbs to a rich form of the mañana syndrome.

Embracing English

Huntington also insists that Mexican immigrants are slow to give up their language. But statistics—and the reality of life in San Antonio—show he's incorrect. It's true that most first-generation immigrants who came here with little education spoke only Spanish. So did the first-generation Germans who came to San Antonio and started a German-language newspaper and their own singing clubs and churches. However, Andy Hernandez, a professor of political science at San Antonio's St. Mary's University, says that his own studies show that by the second generation, 50 percent of Mexican immigrants are dominant in English. In the third generation, 80 percent speak primarily English. According to a Rand Corporation study, Hispanics have the fastest rate of language acquisition of any immigrant group.

In fact, they may be assimilating too well when it comes to the language. The embarrassing secret of many San Antonio Hispanics, including Hernandez, is that they aren't fluent in Spanish. As children, they were discouraged from speaking Spanish at home; their parents told them they wouldn't get ahead. Now, middle class Hispanics don't want to be guilty of what Huntington charges—that they are slow to assimilate. "Anglos have cultural permission to speak Spanish," said Hernandez. "If Latinos speak it, we run the risk of being separatists."

If multiculturalism is the product of immigration in Sonterra, so too is the profound mixing of cultures evident on San Antonio's West Side, which is predominantly Mexican American and poor. Unlike Sonterra's wealthy immigrants, most of the people on the West Side see themselves as underdogs. They view life as los de abajo [those from below]—a phrase used by Tomas Ybarra-Frausto, the associate director of creativity and culture at the Rockefeller Foundation. To drive along streets such as Chihuahua, Trinity, or Guadalupe on the West Side is the opposite of driving in Sonterra. The homes are modest; many are painted in the bold blues, pinks, and greens of Mexican villages. But the streets are crowded with children playing basketball, chattering easily in English and Spanish.

In Sonterra an estimated 40 percent of the subdivision is Hispanic. The West Side is 90 percent Hispanic. If Huntington's theories were true, residents here would value ethnicity above all other interests. As Hispanic as this neighborhood is, both in sensibility and numbers, voters in the last city council election selected an Anglo woman, Patti Radle, over Tom Lopez, a veteran Hispanic politician. They voted their interest, not their ethnicity or nationality. Radle and her husband are well-known antipoverty workers. She speaks Spanish and also sees herself as an underdog. "The people in my neighborhood are not racists," Radle says. "I've lived here for more than thirty years. I knew them and they knew me. When it came down to it, that was more important than color."

Layer upon Layer of Cultures

In truth, the future of a predominantly Hispanic Texas is less likely to reflect the fears of social theorists like Huntington and more likely to resemble present-day San Antonio—messy and complex. The best place to glimpse it is actually downtown, at Alamo Plaza—the same distance from Sonterra as from the West Side. It's not the old mission that's so important but the plaza itself. The shrine is Spanish Colonial in style. The land beneath it is a burial ground for one thousand indigenous mission residents—Indians, in other words. In front of the Alamo stands a Bavarian-style gazebo on one side and the white limestone Cenotaph, designed by Pompeo Luigi Coppini to celebrate the one hundredth anniversary of the Battle of the Alamo, on the other. Contemporary touches include raspa vendors with their carts, along with classically American chain restaurants. On any weekend night, thousands of San Antonio natives and tourists form what approximates a moving conga line from the river, dancing up to the plaza, where magicians perform coin tricks and hip-hop musicians do their things freely borrowing from many genres.

In Alamo Plaza, you do not see just two cultures but layer upon layer of cultures: Spanish, Mexican, English, German, each taking from the others in ways that may not be smooth but are wonderfully surprising. "People expect purity," said Henry Munoz III, a native of San Antonio and the president of Ken Munoz Architects, a firm that's made its name with designs that borrow from all the cultures found in South Texas. "But nothing is pure these days. It's all exuberant, bold, and constantly shifting. That's the future of Texas."

Periodical Bibliography

The following articles have been selected to supplement the diverse views presented in this chapter.

Wes Carter	"The Newspapers Tell Only Half the Story," *Newsweek*, January 13, 2003.
Michael Eric Dyson	"The Content of Their Character," *Other Side*, January/February 2003.
Joe R. Feagin	"Race and Its Continuing Significance on Our Campuses," *Black Issues in Higher Education*, January 16, 2003.
Lawrence H. Fuchs	"Mr. Huntington's Nightmare," *American Prospect*, August 2004.
Earl G. Graves Sr.	"Embracing Diversity, Not Division," *Black Enterprise*, February 2004.
Charlotte Hays	"What Nobody Wants to Say About Race," *Women's Quarterly*, Autumn 2001.
Samuel P. Huntington	"One Nation, Out of Many: Why 'Americanization' of Newcomers Is Still Important," *American Enterprise*, September 2004.
Deroy Murdock	"The Greatest Story Never Told: America's Everyday Racial Harmony," *American Enterprise*, November/December 1998.
Deroy Murdock	"People in the Mirror Are Less Racist than They Appear," *Insight on the News*, November 23, 1998.
Dan Seligman	"How Race Is Written in America," *Commentary*, July 2001.
Earl Shorris	"A Nation of WASPs?" *Nation*, May 31, 2004.
U.S. News & World Report	"The Great Divide," May 28, 2001.
Virginia Whitehouse	"Coverage of Racial Tension," *World & I*, February 2003.
Don Wycliff	"Common Perception of Racism as a Cause of Social Marginality," *Commonweal*, June 1, 2001.

CHAPTER 2

Is Racism a Serious Problem?

Chapter Preface

Assessments of the problem of racism in the United States are anything but clear-cut. With very few exceptions, those who feel that the problem is exaggerated are also willing to admit that it certainly still exists, just as those who feel that racism is a grievous problem are usually willing to concede that some progress has been made.

This ambivalence is reflected in opinion polls about race relations. For example, a February 2003 *Time*/CNN/Harris poll asked Americans, "Do you think race relations in this country will ever get better than they are, or don't you think so?" Sixty-four percent responded "yes, will get better." But this optimism only stretches so far. In a December 2003 Gallup poll that asked "What about the future? Do you think 1) race relations will always be a problem for the United States or 2) a solution for race relations will eventually be worked out?", 63 percent of respondents said that race relations will always be a problem.

Not surprisingly, perceptions about racism are very different among whites, blacks, and Hispanics. In a January 2003 Kaiser poll, 54 percent of blacks said that racism was a major problem in the workplace, compared to 31 percent of Hispanics and 17 percent of whites. Fifty-one percent of blacks felt that racism was a major problem in education, compared to 34 percent of Hispanics and 22 percent of whites. In a January 2002 poll by Public Agenda, 44 percent of blacks reported being "followed around by a store employee because they suspected you were about to shoplift," compared to 30 percent of whites and 10 percent of Hispanics. And in the widest difference of opinion, in a January 1999 poll, 42 percent of blacks felt that they had been stopped by police just because of their race, compared to 11 percent of Hispanics and 6 percent of whites.

Opinion polls are just one way to gain perspective on the issue of racism. The authors in the following chapter examine economic and social indicators as well as anecdotal evidence in their assessments of the problem of racism.

"Discriminatory practices that create heavy costs for African Americans today remain commonplace and pandemic."

Racism Causes Serious Social and Economic Inequality

Joe R. Feagin and Karyn D. McKinney

Joe R. Feagin is a sociologist at Texas A&M University and the author of several books, including *White Racism: The Basics* and *Racist America: Roots, Current Realities, and Future Reparations*. Karyn D. McKinney is a professor of sociology at Penn State University. Together they coauthored *The Many Costs of Racism*, from which the following viewpoint is excerpted. In it, they argue that racism is a major cause of social and economic inequality in the United States. The authors argue that white Americans continue to benefit from slavery and segregation at the expense of African Americans. In addition to detailing the economic disparities between blacks and whites, Feagin and McKinney describe how African Americans face discrimination in the workplace, the criminal justice system, housing, and everyday life.

As you read, consider the following questions:

1. What terms do the authors use to describe white-dominated social networks and organizations that create institutional racism?
2. According to the Department of Defense study cited by the authors, what proportion of black respondents reported encountering racist behavior in the past year?
3. What are the major reasons for continuing racial segregation in housing, in Feagin and McKinney's view?

Joe R. Feagin and Karyn D. McKinney, *The Many Costs of Racism*. Lanham, MD: Rowman & Littlefield Publishers, Inc., 2003. Copyright © 2003 by Rowman & Littlefield Publishers, Inc. Reproduced by permission.

In the late 1960s, [civil rights activists] Kwame Ture and Charles Hamilton made an important distinction between *individual racism*, such as the discriminatory actions of one bigoted white individual, and *institutional racism*, such as the institutional practices that result in large numbers of black children suffering from inadequate nutrition. This distinction is at the core of a deeper understanding of contemporary racism. In most organizations and other societal settings, whites have the ability and opportunity to discriminate as individuals, yet much of their power to harm African Americans or other Americans of color comes from their membership in larger white-dominated social networks and organizations, what have been termed "enforcement coalitions." These white-dominated networks, coalitions, and other organizations typically undergird the discriminatory actions of individual whites. Additionally, even if a white person does not discriminate individually, he or she benefits from white privilege based on group membership.

Institutional Racism

Today, antiblack discrimination is commonplace, recurring, and institutionalized. In many U.S. workplaces, a racial hierarchy of dominant white workers supervising subordinate African Americans is part of the ongoing organization structure. This often lends itself to workplace discrimination of a blatant, subtle, or covert type. In addition, institutionalized racism can be found in the local cultures of organizations—in the informal rules, the implicit protocols for workplace interaction, and the organizational memories. More generally, the racist culture of the larger society—seen in everything from the language of antiblack joking and epithets, to negative media images of black bodies, to distorted accounts of U.S. racial history—constantly interacts with, and reinforces, the social structures of racism. Social psychologist James Jones suggests that cultural racism "comprises the cumulative effects of a racialized worldview, based on belief in essential racial differences that favor the dominant racial group over others." This worldview penetrates most areas of U.S. society. . . .

In the routines of everyday life, the racist and gendered-racist norms imposed by white (or white male) enforcement coalitions are usually linked to, and perpetuated by, the antiblack stereotypes held by the majority of white Americans. Many whites still *think* and *feel* in racialized terms when they choose neighborhoods, mates, employees, and workplace buddies. Prejudice is not simply possessed by individual whites but is "rooted in a sense of group position." Opinion polls and social research demonstrate that antiblack hostility persists among whites today, not because of a few isolated bigots, but because a majority of whites still cling to antiblack stereotypes or images. These images and stereotypes likely lie behind most of the discriminatory actions of whites—who are linked together in white networks and generally dominant in white-controlled workplaces and many other societal settings. . . .

The Costs of Slavery and Legal Segregation

At the center of systemic racism are the many economic and political resources unjustly gained by whites over some fifteen generations since the seventeenth century. This unjust enrichment has included more or less exclusive white access to major social, economic, and political resources that were, until recently, denied to African Americans by slavery and segregation. Think for a moment about the length of time that African Americans have been in North America—largely as the result of involuntary immigration as enslaved workers, beginning 1619. For *nearly two thirds* of their total time in North America, African Americans were enslaved as the *chattel property* of white Americans. From the end of slavery in 1865 until the end of legal segregation in 1968, there was roughly another century of overt and blatant segregation (often a system of near-slavery) for most African Americans. It was only about a third of a century ago that legalized racial oppression of an extreme type was abolished in the United States.

Beginning in the early to mid–seventeenth century, African Americans were brutally and aggressively exploited in a growing, increasingly slavery-centered economic system that brought a range of benefits for white Americans. Over nearly two and a half centuries, millions of enslaved black Americans labored for white slaveholders, large and small. Yet slaveholders were not the only beneficiaries of the slavery system. Those whites who held plantation jobs, those trading in products bought from or sold to plantations, and those working in support sectors such as shipbuilding, banking, and insurance also benefited from the slavery-centered economic system of the long period up to 1865. In this slavery system, many white Americans gained significant income and wealth unjustly, and at a high cost for African Americans. . . .

Kirk. © 1999 by Kirk Anderson. Reproduced by permission.

After slavery, the white majority continued to benefit, directly and indirectly, economically and psychologically, from an extensive system of legal (in the South) and informal (in the North) segregation, a system that lasted in most areas until the 1960s. This white-maintained segregation had physical, psychological, and economic costs for African Americans. These costs involved continuing violence against black men and black women, including widespread police brutality and some six thousand lynchings of African Americans by white lynchers often operating in mobs. Many whites, both men and women and workers at various class levels, gained economically under legal and de facto (informal) segregation. We do not have the space here to demonstrate the substantial economic evidence of white benefits and black costs under legal segregation, so one dramatic illustration will suffice: Millions of white Americans are the contemporary beneficiaries of very large giveaways of federal lands to their farming ancestors. The Homestead Act, passed in the 1860s, eventually provided some 246 million acres at minimal cost for some 1.5 million homesteads. Research by Trina Williams suggests that the number of *current* beneficiaries is perhaps in the range of about 46 million, almost all of whom are white because of restrictions on African American access to such lands during the land-giveaway period that lasted up to about 1930. Until the 1960s, many other federal giveaways of wealth-generating resources—airline routes, radio and television frequencies, mineral resources, and government contracts and licenses—more or less exclusively benefited whites. . . .

Discrimination Today: A Brief Overview

Discriminatory practices that create heavy costs for African Americans today remain commonplace and pandemic. They are found in all major employment sectors. For example, one study in Los Angeles found that about 60 percent of more than a thousand black respondents reported discriminatory barriers in workplaces in just the previous year. Those with more education, like many of our respondents, were *more likely* than those with less income to report such discrimination at their workplaces. In addition, a recent national survey found that more than a third of black respondents reported discrimination in regard to jobs or promotions. Another recent, large-scale survey of forty thousand military personnel by the Department of Defense found that nearly half, or more, of the black respondents had encountered racist jokes, offensive racial discussions, or racial condescension in the last year alone. Significant proportions also had experienced racist comments, racist publications, hostile racial stares, and racial barriers in regard to career-related decisions. Still, employment in the military is considered by many African Americans to mean *fewer* problems with racism than they encounter in the civilian sector.

Reports of unfair racialized treatment by white police officers are commonplace. African American pedestrians and motorists are much more likely than whites to be stopped, questioned, or searched by the police. One urban survey found that black respondents were much more likely than whites to report being unfairly stopped and checked by the police. In addition, one ACLU [American Civil Liberties Union] study of Interstate 95 in Maryland found that, while black drivers made up just 18 percent of those in violation of traffic laws, they were about three quarters of all those stopped and searched by police.

One recent national survey found that more than 80 percent of the black respondents reported facing hostile racial acts in public spaces or public accommodations; these acts by whites included poor service, racial slurs, fearful or defensive behavior, and lack of respect. Another recent survey of 131 black alumni of the University of Florida found that most had been victims of discrimination while traveling. They experienced discrimination while shopping, dining, or staying in a hotel. Nearly eight in ten had experienced discrimination at a restaurant, while about seven in ten reported discrimination in hotels and while shopping. Other major research studies have found serious levels of discrimination for African Americans shopping for new cars, in bail-setting by judges, and in medical treatment by physicians.

Discrimination in Housing

Several recent housing audit studies have found high rates of discrimination for black renters and homebuyers seeking decent housing for themselves and their families. In field research in several cities, when their experiences were compared with those of white test-renters, black test-renters were found to have faced discrimination some 61 to 80 percent of the time depending on the city. For example, a 2001 rental audit study in Houston, using forty paired white and black testers, found that racial discrimination occurred in 80 percent of the attempts to rent by the black testers. This racial mistreatment took the form of openly stated discriminatory policies, misinformation about the housing, and differential treatment in regard to appointments, applications, and terms of contracts. Audit studies have also found discrimination against home buyers. A 2001 Boston audit study included apartment complexes and real estate agencies. In 60 percent of the thirty-five phone and in-person tests, black testers received discriminatory treatment compared to the paired white testers. In addition, a recent national survey asked 1,663 whites about their likely home buying choices. Each white respondent was given a statement asking them to consider how they would react if they were looking for a new house, and found one in their price range that was much better than any other. The researchers then varied what they told the respondents about the racial composition of the hypothetical neighborhood, the quality of local schools, the stability of property values, and the local crime rate. Controlling for other factors, the researchers found that—while the percentage of the neighborhood that was Latino or Asian had no independent effect on white housing choices— the percentage of black people living in the neighborhood, controlling for other factors like crime and school quality, had a strong and independent effect on white housing choices. At low black percentages, the average white respondent would buy the house. However, "after about 15 percent black, net of the variables for which race serves as a proxy, the average white is unlikely to buy the house."

A major reason for the extensive residential segregation along racial lines in U.S. towns and cities lies in the unwillingness of many whites—including the owners of many apartment complexes and many owners or salespeople in real estate firms—to sell or rent to African Americans (especially in historically white residential areas), as well as the unwillingness of many white families to consider housing areas with more than a small percentage of African Americans living there. The consequent residential segregation is a key underlying factor that links to or generates other problems facing African Americans. Segregation of neighborhoods and communities often means, for African Americans, less access to schools with excellent resources, key job networks, quality public services such as hospital care, and quality housing. The latter factor, less access to quality housing, also limits the ability of African American families to build up substantial housing equity, a major source for the wealth passed along by white families now for several generations.

In addition to the most serious and dramatic incidents of racial discrimination, such as being victimized by police brutality, turned down for a job, or excluded from housing, there are the many everyday hassles—the aforementioned "woodwork" discrimination that creates much stress because it is so commonplace. For example, in a recent Detroit study of African American women, researchers found that most of their 331 respondents reported facing everyday types of discrimination—with 62 percent reporting moderate to high levels of this more mundane discrimination. The everyday mistreatment included verbal insults, various types of disrespect, and poor service from whites. Moreover, the consequences of this everyday discrimination were found to be serious; there was a significant relationship between the level of experience with this discrimination and psychological distress.

Economic and Other Social Costs Today

An early 1990s United Nations report discussed the living conditions endured by African Americans compared to people in many other countries around the globe. This report used a Human Development Index (HDI) to measure the quality of life. This index included data on education, income, and life expectancy. Among all of the countries (and major subgroups within countries) examined in the report, U.S. whites, taken separately, ranked *first* in overall quality of life. However, taken separately, African Americans ranked *just thirty-first* in the long list of countries and country subgroups.

Why is there such a huge disparity in quality of life between white and black Americans after three decades of attempts by the federal government to eliminate discrimination and its effects? In the U.S., the remedies for racial discrimination, segregation, and other racial oppression implemented since the 1960s civil rights movements have not brought the significant socioeconomic changes and redistribution that most African Americans and their white and other nonblack allies have long hoped for. Today, there are huge and continuing inequalities in wealth and income between white and black Americans.

We have previously demonstrated that these inequalities are

in part, as the distinguished Supreme Court Justice William O. Douglas once noted in a 1968 court case, the continuing consequences of past racial oppression: "Some badges of slavery remain today. While the institution has been outlawed, it has remained in the minds and hearts of many white men. Cases which have come to this Court depict a *spectacle of slavery unwilling to die.*" In addition, these racial inequalities are in part the legacy of the long era of legal segregation. Black Americans today pay a heavy economic price for centuries of racial oppression, a price perhaps most dear for those with low-wage jobs. Thus, over the last decade or two, black families have had a median family income only about 55 to 63 percent of that of white families. Today, African American families also continue to endure poverty conditions at a much greater rate than white families, and black workers face an unemployment rate that is typically twice that of whites. Black workers are often the first laid off during economic recessions and the last to be recalled. Perhaps more serious is the fact that today, the wealth (net worth) of the average black family is only *about 10 percent*, or so of that of the average white family, a clear indication of the impact of unjust enrichment over many generations—unjust enrichment that has taken the form of privileged if not exclusive white access to critical material, educational, and cultural resources, often for many generations.

"The achievements of black entrepreneurs mostly are overlooked by a mainstream media whose coverage continues to be dominated by stories of blacks mired in poverty."

The Extent of Racial Inequality Is Exaggerated

Steve Miller

Steve Miller is a reporter for the *Washington Times*. In the following viewpoint he argues that black affluence is on the rise and laments that the mainstream media and many blacks are ignoring this trend. Miller provides statistical evidence of black economic and educational progress and profiles several successful black entrepreneurs. The author acknowledges that discrimination exists, but argues that it is far less a problem than it was a generation ago. Miller believes that blacks can best succeed through hard work and determination, and need not rely on affirmative-action policies and government-assistance programs.

As you read, consider the following questions:

1. By what percentage did black-owned businesses increase between 1992 and 1997, according to Miller?
2. Why are blacks making money now, in Miller's view?
3. What narrow definition of being "authentically" black do most people adhere to, according to Lawrence Otis Graham?

The stories pop up like a man-bites-dog piece: "Minority businessman gains foothold . . . Black-owned businesses spread . . . Local black merchant seeing revenue." The headlines almost declare black success an anomaly. It isn't.

Unprecedented strides are being made on the economic ladder in black America. In the 1940s, one in 100 blacks had incomes that approached those of middle-class whites. Today, one in six blacks lives at the poverty line.

Mainstream black magazines such as *Essence* trumpet these triumphs, but most white Americans know well-to-do blacks as athletes and entertainers. Sure, Bob Johnson gets plenty of ink in *Forbes* magazine: The outspoken founder of Black Entertainment Television is a photogenic and articulate man worth more than $2 billion. But what about the Johnson family of Chicago? Johnson Publishing Co., which puts out *Ebony* and *Jet*, is worth more than $450 million.

Black Affluence Is on the Rise

Many in the black community are beginning to resent its conventional image as oppressed and economically disadvantaged. The raw numbers from [the 2000] census show that blacks have made considerable economic and educational progress during the 1990s. Black median household income grew 15 percent between 1989 and 1999, compared with 6 percent for white families; and the number of black-owned firms increased 26 percent from 1992 to 1997, compared with a 7 percent increase for U.S. firms overall.

As consumers, blacks are one of the most targeted markets today. They spend $571 billion annually on consumer goods—$270 billion more than [in 1991]. While travel overall in the United States increased 1 percent between 1997 and 1999, the number of blacks traveling increased by 16 percent during that same period.

Black affluence can be a hard sell, however, especially to those born and raised in poverty. "Anybody who can say they are responsible for their own success is egotistical," insists Wayne Ward Ford, a garrulous, charismatic 50-year-old Iowa legislator. He also is executive director of Urban Dreams, a 16-year-old tax-exempt program for urban youths that he began with $10,000 in seed money from the local city council.

Ford grew up in Washington, where he committed strong-armed robbery and used cocaine, but luckily escaped from a violent world of crime. Now he wrestles with the reality of his success while many in his community still are disadvantaged.

Blair Walker, a journalist who lives in Columbia, Maryland, is even more adamant about the plight of blacks in America. "There are so many families hovering around the poverty level in this country," he says. "Granted, there seems to have been a remarkable boom in black affluence over the past couple of decades. . . ." He trails off, as if perplexed by his own realization.

A Baltimore native, Walker lives comfortably with his wife and two daughters. He is not wealthy, but he is successful. His parents, both schoolteachers, brought him up securely. But Walker still believes his race is not faring well. "A fair number of African-Americans are starting off in the bottom of the eighth inning behind by five runs," he says, his voice flat and determined, the voice of an assured man.

A black America coming apart at the seams is a certainty among people such as Walker, who remain convinced that the destiny of blacks is determined by the legacy of racism. "The difference between a poor white man and a poor black man is that the white man can put on a suit and go to the same arenas as the black and he will be viewed much more positively," Walker says.

But a new generation born after the civil-rights era has realized that corporate doors are wide open and entrepreneurs can be found in all sectors of society, even if old stereotypes die hard. "A story like *Boyz N the 'Hood* sells a lot better than an upper-class entrepreneur who takes care of his family," says Lloyd Lawrence, casually brushing his hand against an $8,000 leisure chair. "There are many more black entrepreneurs than the world knows about."

Lawrence stands in the swank showroom of Roche-Bobois, his furniture boutique in San Francisco's Market District across from Sega headquarters. Lawrence, a former Army captain, rejects outright the rhetoric of black victimhood and oppression. "All my ills were not caused by whites, and I wasn't helped by all African-Americans either," Lawrence says.

In the garage at his Oakland home is an $80,000 Porsche

Turbo he bought recently as a gift to himself. "That was my allowance for working," he explains. "But I don't want to send any Puffy Combs message; I am not interested in ostentatious surroundings." The European furniture he sells is custommade for the rich and famous—people such as Mayor Willie Brown, members of the Oakland Athletics, musicians and computer executives. Lawrence worked at his boutique 11 years before he was able to afford a single piece of furniture from his inventory.

Lawrence's affluence also has brought him a happy family environment. His life revolves around his wife, Cynthia, and his daughter, Ariana. "The most prevalent issue in my household is the education of my daughter," he says. "We give her computer summer camp, world travel. . . . She will have a very well-rounded education."

Overcoming Discrimination

It's a can-do world for Lawrence. "I would be kidding myself to say that I have not been a victim of racism," he says, his face settling into a frown. "But there will always be that person who will reward excellence. While we will never eliminate racism or discrimination, I do delight in proving people wrong."

Blacks are making money now because the business world realizes that buying power is there. The civil-rights movement brought virtually every black with any ambition to the economic table of America. Now, says Herb Strather, "we're part of the American economy, no matter what." Born to welfare recipients in Detroit, Strather eventually brought casino gambling to the Motor City. The self-described philanthropist is a self-made man. He easily can give a $1 million donation to his favorite cause—and he does. He rejects racial set-asides or any system of racial preferences. "I don't want anybody giving me business just because I'm an African-American," Strather says. "All I want is a chance."

The very idea of a handout rankles Tracy Glenn, who grew up in the University City neighborhood of St. Louis, a racially mixed area that now is one of the city's most desirable ZIP codes. Her folks were working class: Dad was employed in a computer job for the government; Mom stayed at home. At 31, the Houston lawyer already has made more money than her parents ever did.

Glenn, who earned her law degree at Boston University, anticipates the collective refrain of people who hear her success story and wonder how someone so privileged can speak to any member of the underclass. "There will be people who say, 'That's easy for her to say, she had a decent upbringing,' but, hey, that's not a reason to sit around and wait for the government or the white man to help them out," Glenn says.

Decrease in the Racial Income Gap Since 1940

Median Annual Incomes of Blacks as a Percent of Those of Whites, 1939–1995

	Males	Female
1940	41	36
1970	59	73
1995	67	89

Stephan Thernstrom and Abigail Thernstrom, *America in Black and White: One Nation, Indivisible.* New York: Simon & Schuster, 1997.

She has been involved in landmark civil-rights cases, representing the white plaintiff in a reverse-discrimination case in Florida. "Discrimination is discrimination; there is no reverse," she says. "I think that most people, and almost all of the people I know, are getting tired of leaning on race. It is who I am," she says, "but it is not what I am."

Andy McLemore Jr. of Detroit is convinced that the long-standing assumptions of the civil-rights establishment are things of the past. He refuses to buy into the prevailing belief that blacks are held back because of a racist white power structure. "I think it is tougher still for blacks, but so many of those limitations are self-imposed," says McLemore, who, with his brother and father, have built a thriving real-estate-development company in Detroit.

A trim man with a stylish mustache and a chuckling, easy manner, McLemore was born in the front room of his grandmother's home in Rocky Mount, North Carolina, and raised in the segregated South. "Back then, they didn't allow black doctors to deliver babies at the hospital," he explains. He lived through the civil-rights era, graduating from Mumford High School in Detroit in 1972 and Wayne State University. The history of second-class citizenship among blacks is not lost on him.

"My grandmother took me around to see the separate drinking fountains and the balconies at the movie theater where the blacks had to sit," McLemore recalls. "It was a different era that I might never have seen, but my grandmother saw to it that I did. I recall she took me to the cotton field across the street and had me touch the cotton boll, to see how hard the shell was."

McLemore has achieved the kind of wealth and luxury that Americans of all races aspire to. Today, he and his family live in a sprawling two-story Tudor house in the ritzy Palmer Woods neighborhood. His garage is full of luxury cars: a black Porsche convertible he bought new in 1997; a white Mercedes with a sunroof; and one of several Land Cruisers with the A-Mac logo on the side.

The Land Cruisers, however, caused a flap in the black community that still rankles McLemore. He bought several of them for his employees to foster team spirit, but some neighbors resented the display of wealth. Not all blacks view success as a good thing, McLemore says. "Many African-Americans feel that because of the color of their skin, they can't achieve something," he says. "They see someone else doing well, and it's jealousy all over."

Stories of Blacks' Success Are Ignored

The achievements of black entrepreneurs mostly are overlooked by a mainstream media whose coverage continues to be dominated by stories of blacks mired in poverty, drugs and inner-city ghettoes rather than comfortable in success, prosperity and wealth. Indeed, blacks who have become successful within the media often help to perpetuate the notion of chronic black underachievement and the problem of racism.

"We continue the struggle," is how TV personality Tavis Smiley opened an appearance at the Georgetown Barnes and Noble bookstore in Washington [in 2001]. Smiley, dapper in a black designer suit over an olive green button-up, sat square-jawed and broad-faced. Unsmiling, he told the crowd that the ordinary routine of living is a fight for most blacks.

"The trouble is that the media look at black people as either the Huxtables or *Boyz N the 'Hood*," sighs Reggie Daniel, president of Scientific & Engineering Solutions, a computer consulting firm in Maryland. "In the end, though, it always falls back on the latter." A youthful looking 41-year-old, Daniel started his firm five years ago with two employees in the basement of his home. He now employees 110 people.

Daniel insists that opportunities for blacks never have been better and are improving every day. "These are not racial issues these days," says Daniel, who came from a blue-collar background in Milwaukee. "These are simply socio-economic issues. And all races have them."

When Lawrence Otis Graham embarked on writing his 1999 book, *Our Kind of People: Inside America's Black Upper Class*, he knew that documenting the existence of a black economic elite would not always be well-received by the black community. "People are uncomfortable with such depictions of blacks," Graham explains. "They have a very narrow definition of being black, where you are only authentic if you are poor, uneducated, listen to rap music and the only way you should make money is to be a rap star or an athlete."

His book was derided by many blacks. Graham himself was labeled an Uncle Tom who ignored the prevalence of racism, inner-city slums and black unemployment. But Graham maintains that black prosperity has every right to sit next to white wealth. "Things are now changing in a number of black communities," he says. "Black families are moving to the suburbs. They now live and work next to white people and send their children to the same schools as white people."

Take, for example, the gated community of Woodmore in Prince George's County, a Maryland suburb that abuts the nation's capital. The dining room of the Country Club at Woodmore is standard upscale, with a sweeping view of the 65-acre lake that is the centerpiece of 18 holes of Arnold Palmer design. The club sits amid a 300-home gated development, a place that might be stereotypically associated with white, Republican churchgoers with minivans and sport utility vehicles in their driveways. In reality, Prince George's

County is the wealthiest black enclave in the United States.

Across the country in Oakland, California, Shannon Reeves slips and tells a "secret" he so far has held tightly: "I will be governor of California one day." In this new decade, it is entirely reasonable that a black Republican could become governor of this Democratic stronghold. This was the state where voters said no to race-based admissions to public universities and colleges, and where Ronald Reagan started his journey to the White House. Despite these populist yet "conservative" milestones, many Californians boast that the state is the starting point for many of the country's progressive causes.

A New Black Leadership?

"Shannon represents the new breed of African-American leader," says Oakland City Manager Robert Bobb, who is black and serves the Democratic leadership in this city of 350,000, which is 38 percent black. "He's smart; he's positive. And there is a bright political future for Shannon that will depend on how he builds coalitions."

His ambition is quintessentially American. The 33-year-old president of the Oakland chapter of the National Association for the Advancement of Colored People (NAACP) means to cast aside race, the ideology of victimhood and the Great Society government programs created during the 1960s—programs, he says, that make people feel comfortable in their poverty. "Yeah, we can ride the bus; yeah, we can go to school; yeah, we can eat in the restaurant," he says. "Can't we move it on from here? I don't see why the media buys this notion of the poor, repressed black."

Reeves was born April 20, 1968, to a 19-year-old mother in Hunter's Point on the San Francisco peninsula, an area riddled with crime and poverty. One of four boys, he was raised by his grandmother in a household that subsisted on food stamps and was bused off to a mostly white school, where he joined the NAACP in junior high. After graduation, he served in the Army and attended Grambling State University in Louisiana.

"I got an internship with Jesse Jackson's 1988 presidential campaign," Reeves says, and received guidance from Representative Maxine Waters of California, among the staunch-est of Democrats. "I was happy as I could be," he admits, watching, learning. "But they were not bringing anything to the table that I wanted."

In 1989, Reeves underwent a change of heart, in part prompted by a political-science teacher who appreciated his reasoning skills, his temperament, his predisposition to iconoclasm. "He asked me if I had ever thought about being a Republican, and I said 'no,'" Reeves recalls. "I said, 'If I go back home as a Republican, they'll run me out of Oakland.'"

Nevertheless, he started debating his friends about GOP goals of lower taxes and limited government. What, he asked them, have Democrats done to help the black man? He con-vinced 75 of his fellow classmates to form the first Republi-can chapter at Grambling.

Today, Reeves is out in the fray, preaching to the uncon-verted. Amid the clatter of dishes at Nellie's soul-food restau-rant in Oakland, he makes one of his trademark, unprovoked pronouncements. "All that I do aggravates black Democratic leaders," he declares. "The black vote is the bedrock of the Democratic Party. People like me are a threat."

No matter how much he disagrees with the NAACP's op-position to free-market capitalism and its embrace of black victimology, however, he remains loyal to the organization that taught him discipline and gave him a home. He has in-creased the membership of the group's Oakland chapter dra-matically, from 900 to 5,000, the West Coast's largest.

Despite this accomplishment, Reeves has angered many in the liberal political establishment. He ran for mayor of Oak-land in 1998, at age 30, and lost to New Age liberal-turned-free-marketer Jerry Brown. The campaign brought out the wolves.

"Shannon Reeves should read our recent black political history a bit more closely, lest he travel the same political trail of Sammy Davis Jr.—functioning as a black yes-man to the white Republicans," Frank Jones wrote in *Gibbs Maga-zine*, the publication of the Gibbs Foundation, an Oakland-based philanthropic organization. "The community is look-ing at him very suspiciously here," Jones later reiterated. "Being a black Republican is a code for being antiblack. It would be different if he were a Democrat; we would have some sort of political control over him."

Rather than being discouraged by his critics, Reeves keeps on pounding the pulpit, urging blacks to embrace the ethic of hard work, personal responsibility and self-help. He answers his critics by saying that the "liberal civil-rights establishment" is attempting to ostracize him because of his maverick Republican views.

"Anytime somebody isn't marching to the beat of the same drum, a black leader steps up to call him on that," he says. "I have so many people come up to me and say, 'You're the only Republican I like.' Once they hear what I'm about, things get easier. They understand ideas like shifting the focus from white racism to responsibility."

"Racial and ethnic minority patients tend to receive a lower quality of care than non-minorities."

Racism Is a Problem in the Health Care System

Institute of Medicine

The Institute of Medicine (IOM) is part of the National Academy of Sciences, a nonprofit organization that advises the federal government and the public on science policy. In 1999 Congress asked the institute to assess the extent of disparities in the quality of health care received by all Americans. In 2002 the IOM released a report concluding that, on average, minorities receive a lower quality of care, even when factors such as income and type of health insurance are accounted for. In the following viewpoint, which is adapted from a summary of its initial report, the IOM highlights the factors—including racial stereotypes and prejudice—behind unequal treatment in the health care system.

As you read, consider the following questions:
1. What is the "downside to stereotyping," according to the IOM?
2. What example does IOM give to illustrate the "self-fulfilling prophecy" that may occur between doctor and patient?
3. What can patients do to avoid inferior health care treatment, according to IOM?

Institute of Medicine, *What Healthcare Consumers Need to Know About Racial and Ethnic Disparities in Healthcare*. Washington, DC: Institute of Medicine, March 2002. Copyright © 2002 by the Institute of Medicine. Reproduced by permission.

It is often difficult to face a visit to the doctor, even if it's just for a routine check-up. Many people find it stressful and even frightening to go to the doctor, especially when they are not feeling well. Worries about starting treatment for an illness or disease can get worse when people think about how much the treatment will cost and the possibility of the doctor making a mistake. And for minority patients, there can be more issues to think about—including whether their race or ethnicity will affect the kind of care they receive.

Racial and Ethnic Gaps in Access to Health Care

There are wide differences between racial and ethnic groups in access to health care and the availability of health insurance. Minorities, especially Hispanic and African-American families, are less likely than whites to have private health insurance. Or if they have insurance, minorities are more likely than whites to be enrolled in health plans that place tight limits on the types of services that patients may receive. Also, the best quality health care services and providers are not always found in minority communities. These are some of the major reasons why minorities receive a lower quality of care.

But recent medical research also shows that racial and ethnic minority patients tend to receive a lower quality of care than non-minorities, even when they have the same types of health insurance.

For that reason, Congress asked the Institute of Medicine (IOM) to investigate racial and ethnic disparities in health care delivery. The IOM was instructed to determine how wide the health care gap is, identify potential reasons why it occurs, and suggest ways to eliminate it. In its final report (*Unequal Treatment: Confronting Racial and Ethnic Disparities in Healthcare*), the panel of scientists and doctors assembled by the IOM concluded that minority patients are less likely than whites to receive the same quality of heath care, even when they have similar insurance or the ability to pay for care. To make matters worse, this health care gap is linked with higher death rates among minorities.

The IOM report defined health care *disparities* as differences in the quality of care received by minorities and non-minorities who have equal access to care—that is, when these groups have similar health insurance and the same access to a doctor—*and* when there are no differences between these groups in their preferences and needs for treatment. This definition acknowledges that some differences in the quality of health care between minorities and whites are explainable. For example, research shows that some minority patients are more likely than whites to reject their doctor's advice for treatment, although this difference in treatment preferences is generally very small.

The Causes of Health Care Disparities

The IOM report found that health care disparities do not have one simple cause. Instead, many potential sources of health care disparities were discovered. Three of these sources are described below.

The way health care systems are organized and operate can contribute to differences. Sometimes health care systems, hospitals, or clinics adopt policies or practices that are based on good intentions—such as the need to contain health care costs— but may pose barriers to minority patients' ability to access care. For example, some health plans offer financial incentives to physicians to keep costs low. Keeping health care costs down is important, but these policies may unintentionally hurt minorities, in that cost-savings may come at the expense of patients who are least educated about their treatment options and least likely to push their doctor for more services.

In addition, many health plans do not offer professional interpretation or translation services to patients that don't speak English. Professional interpretation and translation services are important to help non-English speaking patients fully participate in treatment decisions and discuss concerns with their doctor privately.

Patients' attitudes and behaviors can contribute to disparities. There is some evidence that patients' attitudes may contribute to disparities. Some minority patients do not trust health care professionals, and therefore may put off seeing a doctor until their illness is too far along to effectively treat. Others do not follow their doctor's instructions exactly. In addition, some evidence suggests that minority patients are more likely to reject or refuse their doctor's recommendations for treatment. Studies show, however, that this represents only a small percentage of minority patients, and that minorities are only slightly more likely than white patients to refuse recommended treatment.

Racial Bias Among Doctors

Racial bias is [an] important source of the differences in the ways life-threatening diseases are treated. Recent evidence suggests that racial stereotyping, and even discrimination, influence doctors' treatment recommendations for patients. [Researcher] K. Schulman and his colleagues asked doctors to respond to videotaped interviews with "patients" who were actually actors with identical medical histories and symptoms. Only the race and gender of the actors were different. Doctors turned out to be significantly less likely to refer black women for aggressive treatment of cardiac symptoms than other categories of patients with the same symptoms. Doctors were also asked about their perceptions of patients' personal characteristics. Black male actor-patients, whose symptoms and comments were identical to white male actor-patients, were perceived to be less intelligent, less likely to participate in treatment decisions, and more likely to miss appointments. Doctors in the study thought that both black men and women would be less likely to benefit from invasive procedures than their white counterparts, less likely to comply with doctors' instructions, and more likely to come from low socioeconomic backgrounds. In other words, where actor-patients were identical except for race, black patients were usually seen as low-income members of an inferior group.

Michael K. Brown et al., *Whitewashing Race: The Myth of a Color-Blind Society*. Berkeley: University of California Press, 2003.

Finally, there is evidence that *health care providers' biases, prejudices, and uncertainty when treating minorities can contribute to health care disparities.* This summary focuses on how providers' attitudes and beliefs—even those that they aren't consciously aware of—may influence the quality of patient care, and what patients can do about it.

Doctors' Uncertainty

To understand how doctors may contribute to health care disparities, it's important to understand how they make decisions about patient care. Many of the decisions that doctors must make are made with a degree of uncertainty. This uncertainty can be related to the patient's diagnosis, how the patient may respond to treatment, whether treatment might lead to potential complications, or even the patient's long-term outlook. To make matters worse, in many health care settings doctors may face significant time pressures, resource constraints, and on occasion, complex medical problems that are not easily understood or solved.

Uncertainty can therefore make finding the right diagnosis and treatment plan a challenge for any doctor. But when faced with patients who are from different racial or ethnic backgrounds, doctors may find that their uncertainty about the patient's condition and best course of treatment is even greater. A doctor may be uncertain about how a particular disease (or treatment) will progress in a minority group. A patient's test results may not point to an obvious solution. Sometimes, patients don't know how to describe their symptoms, or they are nervous or embarrassed about them. In addition, many doctors don't talk to their patients in plain language; they use medical terms that are difficult to understand. These kinds of problems can lead to greater uncertainty when doctors and patients don't share the same background. And in many communities, there are additional language barriers—the doctor and patient may not speak the same language, and many health care systems do not employ interpreters. Also, there can be cultural misunderstandings that are separate from language problems—a patient's understanding of his or her illness may be different from a doctor's perspective. Each of these factors increases the doctor's uncertainty about what care a patient may need. The result may be that the diagnosis and treatment plan may not be well suited to the patient's needs.

Stereotypes, Bias, and Prejudice

Stereotyping is a process by which people use social groups (such as sex and race) to gather, process, and recall information about other people. Stereotypes are, in other words, labels that we give to people on the basis of what groups we think they belong to.

Most people think of the word "stereotype" as a negative one, but actually these labels can be useful. Stereotyping helps people to organize a very complex world. Using them can give us more confidence in our abilities to understand a situation and respond to it. There is, however, a downside to stereotyping. It is the nature of stereotypes to be biased or unfair. They carry some level of judgment—this judgment can be positive or negative. For example, one African-American patient who had been diagnosed with diabetes reported a very negative experience. While writing a prescription, the doctor told her, "I need to write this prescription for these pills, but you'll never take them and you'll come back and tell me you're eating pig's feet and everything. . . ." Clearly, this provider looked at this person's race and assumed she had a certain type of diet and would therefore ignore his advice.

It is easy to recognize negative stereotypes, such as the kinds of attitudes that we associate with bigotry. But almost everyone stereotypes others, even though most people don't even realize they do it. And, unfortunately, we live in a society that is still affected by negative attitudes between different racial and ethnic groups. So even people who would never endorse explicitly biased stereotypes—who truly believe that they do not judge others based on social categories—have been unconsciously influenced by the *implicitly* biased stereotypes in American society.

Stereotypes May Influence Medical Decisions

Both implicit and explicit stereotypes shape our personal interactions. They affect how we recall information and guide our expectations and perceptions. The subtle clues we give about our own stereotypes—and how we interpret those given by others—can even produce "self-fulfilling prophecies" in social situations. That is, our own beliefs about how a situation should or will unfold can actually influence the interaction so that it meets our expectations. For example, a doctor's conscious or subconscious stereotypes about whether minority patients will stick to treatment plans or keep follow-up appointments can convey the message that the doctor doesn't expect the patient to cooperate.

Prejudice can also affect the quality of health care that minorities receive. Prejudice is defined as an unjustified negative attitude based on a person's group membership. Such a negative attitude is often revealed through explicitly biased stereotypes. It is a sad fact that the majority of white Americans hold prejudicial attitudes about minorities. Survey results indicate that as many as one-half to three-quarters of whites believe minorities are less intelligent, prefer to live on welfare, or are more prone to violence than white people. Yet most of these people do not recognize their attitudes as prejudice.

It's likely that most health care providers are not overtly prejudiced. After all, they have dedicated their lives to helping people stay well. But like many people, health care providers may not recognize evidence of prejudice in their own behavior.

There Are Ways to Correct These Disparities

It may seem like an unbreakable cycle, but it is not a hopeless situation. The first step toward correcting the problem is to make people aware of it. Surveys show that, by and large, the general public is unaware that minorities receive a lower quality of care than whites. Many physicians, too, are unaware of the extent of racial and ethnic disparities in care. Greater awareness is likely to lead to more public and professional concern to solve the problem.

Awareness of the problem is not enough, however, to eliminate health care disparities. Wide-ranging strategies need to be aimed at state and federal health policy, policies and practices of health systems, and training of health care providers. These strategies should be developed and put into place at the same time. Addressing only one strategy at a time will not solve the problem.

For example, health care systems can take steps to help minority patients to better access care and make sure that high quality care is provided to all patients. In communities where there are a large number of people that prefer to use languages other than English, translation services can help patients feel more comfortable and that their needs are being heard. Health care systems can also take steps to improve relationships between doctors and patients. If each patient has a specific provider that they are able to see when they need care, the two are often able to overcome cultural barriers. This may help patients trust their provider and feel confident in following medical advice

Education is also important. First, doctors and other health care providers have to recognize that disparities exist, despite their best intentions. More importantly, doctors and other providers should receive *cross-cultural education.* This kind of training is designed to teach providers how cultural and social factors influence health care. It helps providers understand how to interact with patients who have different cultural points of view in general and, in particular, different attitudes about health care. It also helps providers talk to and interact with these patients in a more effective way.

Patients Can Make a Difference in Their Own Care

Patients can also make positive changes. There is some evidence to show that patient education efforts can make a difference. Books, pamphlets, and Internet sites teach patients what to expect during exams and provide information about communicating with providers. When patients are able to ask questions and get answers they understand, they are able to participate in making medical decisions. Providing patient education materials is an important step for health care systems; using them is an important step for patients.

"Inferring discrimination from the existence of disparities is a divisive distraction."

The Problem of Racism in the Health Care System Is Exaggerated

Sally Satel and Jonathan Klick

Sally Satel is a psychiatrist and the author of *PC, M.D.: How Political Correctness Is Corrupting Medicine*, and Jonathan Klick is an assistant professor of law at Florida State University. In the following viewpoint they argue that while there are differences in the health care received by different ethnic and racial groups, there is little evidence that these differences are due primarily to racism on the part of health care providers. For example, they argue, variances in income, education, and type of health insurance could account for many of the differences. Klick and Satel note that physicians do sometimes take race into account when it is clinically appropriate to do so, and that in some cases patients who receive fewer tests and treatments have better health outcomes.

As you read, consider the following questions:

1. What were the controversial changes to the executive summary of the 2003 HHS report on health care disparities, according to the authors?
2. What is "defensive medicine" and how might it influence health care disparities, in the authors' opinion?
3. What reasoning underlies racial preferences in medical school admissions, according to Klick and Satel?

J ust before Christmas [2003] the Department of Health and Human Services [HHS] released the National Healthcare Disparities Report. It documents an all-too-familiar problem in public health: the poorer health status of individuals on the lower rungs of the socioeconomic ladder and the fact that they often receive different treatment than those with more resources and higher education.

An Overblown Controversy

The term disparity, though, refers not just to differences. Over the last few years it has acquired another connotation in public health circles, referring to differences in care determined by ethnicity. And therein lies the potential for race politics. In mid-January [2004], those politics surfaced. "Racial Disparities Played Down; At Request of Top Officials, Report on Health Care Differs from Draft," ran an article in the *Washington Post*. At issue were changes to the executive summary of the HHS report. These included using the more neutral word difference instead of disparity; removing statements that disparities are "national problems" that are "pervasive" and exact a "personal and societal price"; and the substitution of some examples of health differences in which minorities fare better than the general population for those depicting minorities as doing worse.

On January 13 [2004], Henry Waxman, ranking minority member of the House Government Reform Committee, sent a scathing letter to HHS Secretary Tommy Thompson protesting these prepublication changes. The substance of the roughly 200-page report, brimming with documented differences in health status and treatment, was not at issue—simply the summary—yet Waxman warned Thompson that the changes "alter the report's meaning . . . and fit a pattern of the manipulation of science by the Bush Administration." An accompanying press release, signed by members of the Congressional Black Caucus, Congressional Asian Pacific American Caucus, and Congressional Hispanic Caucus, claimed that "by tampering with the conclusions of its own scientists, HHS is placing politics before social justice."

Further context for the "tampering" charge was provided by H. Jack Geiger, an emeritus professor of community medicine at the City University of New York. His January 27 op-ed in the *Washington Post* ("Why Is HHS Obscuring a Health Care Gap?") praised a 2002 report from the Institute of Medicine, "Unequal Treatment: Confronting Racial and Ethnic Disparities in Health," to which he was a contributor. That report suggested that racial differences in health care are "rooted in historic and contemporary inequities" and asserted that "stereotyping," "prejudice," and "bias" by doctors, hospitals, and other care providers contribute to the disparities.

Having seen both versions of the executive summary of the HHS report, we agree that the earlier one was more powerful and detailed. (Indeed, on February 10, Thompson agreed to release the executive summary in its original form, saying that a "mistake" was made.) But the contents of the full report were never disputed, and there is little reason to worry that HHS is downplaying the disparity issue. "Eliminating health care differences resulting from unequal opportunities must continue to be a public policy priority," says the HHS report within the first few pages. Nevertheless, the report's critics perceived the revision as a malign effort, in Geiger's words, "to avoid the truth"—namely, that gaps in treatment are also the product of racial discrimination in the health care system. More than a thousand studies, Geiger insists, document "inequities" in the health care provided for minorities.

Inequities? Not so fast—especially since "inequity," as Geiger has made clear in his writings on race and health, implies inferior care based solely on the patient's race. Let's be clear about what those studies do show, bearing in mind that the vast majority of them—which were assembled by Physicians for Human Rights with Dr. Geiger's assistance—are not sufficiently detailed to even begin to illuminate the recesses of the treatment gap.

A Complex Issue

The most rigorous studies control for numerous variables that could explain why minorities are less likely to undergo procedures such as cardiac catheterization—variables such as other illnesses that might make the procedure inadvisable. But because most of the disparity studies rely upon review of hospital charts or large Medicare databases, they cannot take into account such important factors as patient preferences or supplemental insurance. Nor do they reveal how doctors made their treatment decisions.

Poverty, Not Racism, Is the Problem

Researchers at Manhattan's Memorial Sloan-Kettering Cancer Center and the Center for the Study of Health Care Change in Washington [have shown] that white and black patients, on average, do not even visit the same population of physicians—making the idea of preferential treatment by individual doctors a far less compelling explanation for disparities in health. They show, too, that a higher proportion of the doctors that black patients tend to see may not be in a position to provide optimal care. . . .

The research team, led by Dr. Peter Bach, examined more than 150,000 visits by black and white Medicare recipients to 4,355 primary-care physicians nationwide in 2001. It found that the vast majority of visits by black patients were made to a small group of physicians—80% of their visits were made to 22% of all the physicians in the study. . . .

Physicians of any race who disproportionately treat African-American patients, the study notes, were less likely to have passed a demanding certification exam in their specialty than the physicians treating white patients. More important, they were more likely to answer "not always" when asked whether they had access to high-quality colleague-specialists to whom they could refer their patients (e.g., cardiologists, gastroenterologists), or to nonemergency hospital services, diagnostic imaging and ancillary services such as home health aid.

These patterns reflect geographic distribution. Primary-care physicians who lack board certification and who encounter obstacles to specialized services are more likely to practice in areas where blacks receive their care—namely, poorer neighborhoods, as measured by the median income.

Sally Satel, "The Care Is Colorblind," *OpinionJournal.com*, August 6, 2004.

Then there is the matter of rational inference. Physicians base their clinical decisions on experience and statistical norms. These are sometimes influenced by race (or sex or class, for that matter). But judgments that appear to be made on race may actually be made on other variables that simply correlate with race. Level of education is such a variable. As recent work by Dana Goldman and James Smith of RAND shows, adherence to treatment regimens in patients with HIV and diabetes varied greatly with the patient's level of schooling.

In practical terms, if a physician thinks that a patient will not comply with triple therapy for HIV, he might either forgo the medication or give the patient a compliance "trial," wherein the patient must at least keep a second appointment in order to receive medication. To the extent that a physician does the former without strong clinical justification, he has acted unethically. At the same time, failure to draw rational inferences about patients—especially the likelihood of their taking potent medications properly or caring for surgical wounds once discharged from the hospital—can lead to worse health outcomes for minority and white patients alike. A conscientious doctor cannot simply prescribe complicated therapies and hope for the best.

For doctors, data about health care disparities serve a consciousness-raising function, prompting them to ask themselves whether they are giving every patient the opportunity to benefit from treatment. But to elevate the phenomenon of making clinical generalizations to the level of a civil-rights violation is a huge leap—yet one the disparity-equals-racism crowd is eager to make.

More Is Not Always Better

Research in health disparities often boils down to the assumption that more is always better. Consider: A 1999 study from Memorial Sloan Kettering Cancer Center found that black patients with operable lung cancer underwent surgery for removal of part of the lung less often than whites. Insurance coverage was not a factor. Five years later one quarter of the black patients, and one-third of whites, were still alive, strongly suggesting that surgery would have saved many black lives. (Even so, this was a study based on Medicare records and a National Cancer Institute database, so there were clinical subtleties—for example, results of pulmonary function tests and patients' desire for the operation—that remained unknown and could have affected the picture.)

But differences in care do not inevitably translate into differences in outcome. In fact, according to a Kaiser Family Foundation review of cardiac care studies, the overwhelming majority found no mortality differences between races despite lower rates of procedures for blacks. One possible explanation is that catheterization may be overused in white patients, meaning that the procedure is performed even when it will probably not benefit patients.

Often, such overuse of procedures is the result of nonclinical influences. For example, numerous researchers have documented the practice of "defensive medicine," in which physicians provide care with infinitesimal or nonexistent expected benefits solely to protect themselves from liability in subsequent legal proceedings. This research shows that doctors facing lower liability exposure thanks to state medical malpractice law reforms perform fewer procedures and clinical tests with no adverse effects on patient health. This implies that a doctor's expectations of future litigation will influence his care decisions. If different racial groups have different propensities to sue, or if eventual judgments are correlated with race, care disparities will arise, but it is not clear that those disparities have any consequences for patient health.

Such socioeconomic complexities are too often ignored in the debates over health care disparities, where insinuations of racism are a sure media draw. This is unfortunate, since constructive policy proposals require a reliable diagnosis. Yet many medical schools, health philanthropies, policymakers, and politicians are proceeding as if "bias" were an established fact.

Minorities' Access to Quality Care

For example, there is now a "cultural competence training" industry that, among other activities, has been known to conduct patronizing racial sensitivity training for doctors. This is not to be confused with the need to learn the local anthropology of unacculturated populations, a vital necessity for physicians who work with cultural minorities. In addition, medical schools are forthright in lowering academic and performance standards in the service of building a more racially diverse workforce. The main rationale for these racial preferences is to take advantage of the fact that minority doctors are more likely to practice in underserved areas and to fulfill the (unfounded) premise that minority patients overwhelmingly prefer same-race doctors. Yet a more fair and clinically responsible way to get good doctors into poor neighborhoods is to offer financial incentives.

Inferring discrimination from the existence of disparities is a divisive distraction from the factors that have undisputed and sizable influence on disparity: access to care, quality of care, and health literacy. When access to care is excellent and quality of care and patient characteristics are relatively homogeneous—such as in military health care systems—there are negligible racial disparities in care.

The HHS report on health care disparities rightly attacks the disparity issue as a socioeconomic problem tied to access to quality care and to the health literacy of potential patients. There was no "papering over" of health care differences, as its critics allege. If anything, to say that the differences—which are real and surely need attention—are born substantially of racial discrimination in the health care system is the true manipulation of the science.

Periodical Bibliography

The following articles have been selected to supplement the diverse views presented in this chapter.

Business Week	"Racism in the Workplace," July 30, 2001.
John Derbyshire	"In Defense of Racial Profiling: Where Is Our Common Sense?" *National Review*, February 19, 2001.
Economist	"Them; the Origins of Racism," December 15, 2001.
Economist	"Thinking About It; Racial Prejudice," November 22, 2003.
Robert Kuttner	"Having It Both Ways on Race," *American Prospect*, January 13, 2003.
Deroy Murdock	"Biased Media Distort the Truth About Supposed Racism of Police," *Insight on the News*, May 21, 2001.
Michele Orecklin	"The Role of Race," *Time*, August 28, 2003.
Rick Reilly	"White Like Me," *Sports Illustrated*, February 4, 2004.
Sally Satel	"The Indoctrinologists Are Coming," *Atlantic Monthly*, January 2001.
Deral Wing Sue	"Dismantling the Myth of a Color-Blind Society," *Black Issues in Higher Education*, November 6, 2003.
Stuart Taylor Jr.	"Finding Racial Bias Where There Was None," *National Journal*, June 9, 2001.
Time	"What's Race Got to Do with It?" July 30, 2001.
John Edgar Wideman	"Whose War: The Color of Terror," *Harper's Weekly*, March 2002.
Patricia J. Williams	"State of Denial," *Nation*, October 13, 2003.
Raymond A. Winbush	"Back to the Future: Campus Racism in the Twenty-First Century," *Black Collegian*, October 2001.

CHAPTER 3

What Should Government Do to Improve Race Relations?

Chapter Preface

In December 2000 the U.S. Census Bureau released the first results of the census that had been completed a few months earlier, announcing, "Never have we been so diverse; never have we been so many; never have we been so carefully measured." In measuring America's diversity, the census reflects centuries-old controversies over how the U.S. government should deal with race.

Every census after 1790 has classified the population based on race, but the categories have changed almost every decade. In 1870 the categories were white, black, mulatto, Chinese, and Indian. For most of the twentieth century, the categories were white, black, American Indian, Asian, and "other race." Former Census Bureau director Kenneth Prewitt notes that "Mexican first appeared in 1930, but was quickly dropped when the government of Mexico complained Mexican was not a race. Mexicans were then counted as white until 1970, when Hispanic origin appears on the census form as an ethnic rather than a racial category."

The shifting census categories reflect disagreements and changing attitudes about what race is and whether or how it differs from ethnicity and country of origin. For every census there have been individuals who felt the classifications did not reflect their true identities, either because they were of mixed ancestry or because their appearance did not meet stereotypical expectations.

The 2000 census attempted to address this by, for the first time, allowing individuals to select multiple races and ethnicities—to "mark one more" on the census questionnaire—to describe themselves. With sixty-three racial categories and the extra classification of Hispanic–Not Hispanic, the census now has 126 race-ethnic groups. The result is a much more complicated picture of America's diversity. By moving beyond a simplistic racial taxonomy, Prewitt believes that "'Mark one more' opens the door to a postracial future." The authors in the following chapter offer opinions on how the government should address the complex race relations that have resulted from America's increasing diversity.

"Martin Luther King, Jr., hoped for a color-blind society, but only as oppression and racism were destroyed."

Race Should Be a Consideration in Public Policy

Michael Eric Dyson

Michael Eric Dyson is an ordained Baptist minister, a professor of humanities at the University of Pennsylvania, and author of several books on race. The following viewpoint is adapted from his book, *I May Not Get There with You: The True Martin Luther King Jr.* In it, Dyson takes issue with conservatives who have cited Martin Luther King Jr.'s vision of a color-blind society in their calls for an end to affirmative action and other policies aimed at reducing racial inequality. Dyson maintains that while King hoped that society would some day achieve racial equality and become "blind" to race, he also believed that until that dream was achieved, government had a responsibility to help disadvantaged groups, including minorities. Dyson warns that by pretending that racial equality has already been achieved and seeking to ban race-conscious government policies, conservatives are exacerbating America's racial problems.

As you read, consider the following questions:

1. What thirty-four words have conservative leaders appropriated in their opposition to affirmative action, in the author's view?
2. What governmental remedy for slavery and black oppression did King propose in his book *Why We Can't Wait*, according to Dyson?

Michael Eric Dyson, "The Content of Their Character," *The Other Side*, vol. 39, January/February 2003. Copyright © 2003 by *The Other Side*. Reproduced by permission of the author.

"I am a mother with six kids," says the beautiful ebony-skinned woman adorned in batik-print African dress and silver loop earrings. "And part of the time I don't even know where I'm going to get the next meal for my children."

All Martin Luther King, Jr., can do is shake his head and utter, "My, my."

King was on a 1968 swing through rural, poor parts of the Black South, drumming up support for his Poor People's March on Washington later that year. He had stopped at a small white wood-frame church in Mississippi to press his case, and to listen to the woes of the poor. A painting of a White Jesus, nearly ubiquitous in Black churches, observed their every move. Later King would absorb more tales of Mississippi's material misery. "I want you to know that you have my moral support," King compassionately told those he met. "I'm going to be praying for you. I'm going to be coming back to see you, and we are going to be demanding, when we go to Washington, that something be done and done immediately about these conditions."

King couldn't keep that promise; his life would be snuffed out a mere three weeks before his massive campaign reached its destination. But King hammered home the rationale behind his attempt to unite the desperately poor. He understood that the government owed something to the masses of Black folk who had been left behind as America parceled out land and money to Whites while exploiting Black labor.

"At the very same time that America refused to give the Negro any land," King argues, "through an act of Congress our government was giving away millions of acres of land in the West and the Midwest, which meant it was willing to undergird its White peasants from Europe with an economic floor.

"But not only did they give them land," King's indictment speeds on, "they built land-grant colleges with government money to teach them how to farm. Not only that, they provided county agents to further their expertise in farming. Not only that, they provided low interest rates in order that they could mechanize their farms.

"Now, when we come to Washington in this campaign, we are coming to get our check."

Misrepresenting King's Vision

This is not the King whom conservatives have used to undermine progressive politics and Black interests. Indeed, conservatives in this country must be applauded for their perverse ingenuity in co-opting the legacy of Martin Luther King, Jr., and the rhetoric of the civil rights movement. Unlike the radical Right, whose racist motivations are hardly obscured by painfully infrequent references to racial equality, contemporary conservatives often speak of race in moral terms gleaned from the Black freedom struggle. Thus, while the radical Right is open about its disdain for social upheaval in the sixties, many conservatives pretend to embrace a revolution that they, in fact, bitterly opposed.

This is especially troubling because of the moral assault by conservatives on civil rights activists who believe that affirmative action, for instance, is part of the ongoing attack on discrimination. These same conservatives rarely target the real enemies of racial equality: new-fangled racists who drape their bigotry in scientific jargon or political demagoguery. Instead, they huff stigma at civil-rights veterans who risked great peril to destroy a racist virus found even in the diseased body of ultra-conservatism. Perhaps most insidious, conservatives rarely admit that whatever racial enlightenment they possess likely came as Blacks and their allies opposed the conservative ideology of race.

Worse still, when the civil-rights revolution reached its zenith and accomplished some of its goals—including recasting the terms in which the nation discussed race—many conservatives recovered from the shock to their system of belief by going on the offensive. The 1960s may have belonged to the liberals, but the subsequent decades have been whipped into line by a conservative backlash. After eroding the spirit of liberal racial reform, conservatives have breathed new life into the racial rhetoric they successfully forced the liberals to abandon. Now terms like "equal playing field," "racial justice," "equal opportunity," and, most ominous, "color-blind" drip from the lips of formerly stalwart segregationist politicians, conservative policy wonks, and intellectual hired guns for deep-pocketed right-wing think tanks. Crucial concepts are deviously turned inside out, leaving the impression of a cyclone turned in on itself. Affirmative action is rendered as reverse racism, while goals and timetables are remade, in sinister fashion, into "quotas."

Attitudes Toward Black and Latino Economic Progress by Race

	Attitudes Regarding African Americans		Attitudes Regarding Latino Americans	
	According to		*According to*	
	Blacks	*Whites*	*Latinos*	*Whites*
Opportunities available:				
More than whites	1%	13%	6%	11%
Less than whites	74	27	61	32
About the same	23	58	28	54
Discrimination faced:				
A lot	48	20	28	15
Some	39	51	59	49
Little	9	17	16	24
None	2	8	5	9
Income:				
Better off than whites	9	4	11	5
Worse off than whites	73	57	60	68
About the same	15	38	27	26
Access to health care:				
Better off than whites	9	11	15	6
Worse off than whites	61	35	50	46
About the same	26	50	33	42
Types of jobs:				
Better off than whites	9	6	12	6
Worse off than whites	67	49	61	65
About the same	23	44	27	27

"Washington Post/Kaiser Foundation/Harvard University Racial Attitudes Survey," *Washington Post*, July 11, 2001.

This achievement allows the conservatives to claim that they are opposed to the wrong-headed results of the civil rights movement, even as they claim to uphold its intent— racial equality. Hence, conservatives seize the spotlight and appear to be calm and reasonable about issues of race. In their shadows, liberals and leftists are often portrayed as unreasonable and dishonest figures who uproot the grand ideals of the civil rights movement from its moral ground.

At the heart of the conservative appropriation of King's vision is the argument that King was an advocate of a color-blind society. Hence, any policy or position that promotes color consciousness runs counter to King's philosophy. Moreover, affirmative action is viewed as a poisonous rejection of King's insistence that merit, not race, should determine how education and employment are distributed. The wellspring of such beliefs about King is a singular, golden phrase lifted from his "I Have a Dream" speech. "I have a dream," King eloquently yearned, "my four little children will one day live in a nation where they will not be judged by the color of their skin but by the content of their character." Of the hundreds of thousands of words that King spoke, few others have had more impact than these thirty-four, uttered when he was thirty-four years old, couched in his most famous oration. Tragically, King's American dream has been seized and distorted by a group of conservative citizens whose forebears and ideology have trampled King's legacy.

A Distant Dream

Conservatives and liberals alike have feasted on King's hunger for a world beyond race, a world where color will be neither the final sign of human identity nor the basis for enjoying advantage or suffering liability. To be sure, King's life and work pointed to such a day when his dream might be fulfilled. But he was too sophisticated a racial realist, even as he dreamed in edifying technicolor in our nation's capital, to surrender a sobering skepticism about how soon that day might arrive. His religious faith worked against such naivete since it held that evil can be conquered only by acknowledging its existence. King never trusted the world to harness the means to make itself into the utopia of which even his brilliant dream was a faint premonition.

The problem with many of King's conservative interpreters (including Black conservatives, like Shelby Steele and Ward Connerly) is not simply that they have not been honest about how they have consciously or unintentionally hindered the realization of King's dream, but more brutally that in the face of such hindrances, they have demanded that we act as if the dream has become real and has altered the racial landscape. As an ideal, the color-blind motif spurs us to develop a nation where race will make no difference. As a presumed achievement, color-blindness reinforces the very racial misery it is meant to replace.

Martin Luther King, Jr., has wrongly been made the poster boy for opposition to affirmative action. His glittering moral authority has been liberally sprinkled on conservative assaults on civil rights communities and progressive Black interests, all because of thirty-four words lifted out of the context of his commitment to complete equality and freedom for all Americans. Rarely has so much depended on so little. But to take full and just measure of King's views, we must read him, studying his words and his life as he evolved to engage the myriad forces that hinder the liberation of Black and poor people.

King's Vision of Racial Reparation

Unfortunately, King has been used to chide Black and other humanitarian leaders who have sought, however imperfectly, to extend the views that he really held. If conservatives were to read and listen to King carefully, they would not only find little basis in King's writings to justify their assaults in his name, but they would be brought up short by his vision of racial compensation and racial reparation, a vision far more radical than most current views of affirmative action.

King wrote in *Why We Can't Wait* that few "people consider the fact that, in addition to being enslaved for two centuries," that Black folk were also robbed of wages for toil. "No amount of gold could provide an adequate compensation for the exploitation and humiliation of the Negro in America down through the centuries," he continued. "Not all the wealth of this affluent society could meet the bill. Yet a price can be placed on unpaid wages. The ancient common law has always provided a remedy for the appropriation of the labor of one human being by another. This law should be made to apply for American Negroes. The payment should be in the form of a massive program by the government of special, compensatory measures which could be regarded as a settlement in accordance with the accepted practice of common law." He proposed a governmental remedy modeled on the G.I. Bill of Rights—"a broad-based and gigantic Bill of Rights for the Disadvantaged, our veterans of the long siege of denial."

King ingeniously anticipated objections to programs of racial compensation on the grounds that they discriminated against poor Whites who were equally disadvantaged. He knew that conservatives would manipulate racial solidarity through an insincere display of new-found concern for poor Whites that pitted their interests against those of Blacks. King claimed that "millions of White poor" would benefit from the bill. Although he believed that the "moral justification for special measures for Negroes is rooted in the robberies inherent in the institution of slavery," many poor Whites, he argued, were "the derivative victims" of slavery. He conceded that poor whites are "chained by the weight of discrimination" even if its "badge of degradation does not mark them." King understood how many poor Whites failed to understand the class dimensions of their exploitation by elite Whites who appealed to vicious identity politics to obscure their actions. King held that discrimination was in ways "more evil for [poor whites], because it has confused so many by prejudice that they have supported their own oppressors." Hence, it was only just that a Bill of Rights for the Disadvantaged, intent on "raising the Negro from backwardness," would also rescue "a large stratum of the forgotten white poor."

Martin Luther King, Jr., hoped for a color-blind society, but only as oppression and racism were destroyed. Then, when color suggested neither privilege nor punishment, human beings could enjoy the fruits of our common life.

Until then, King realized—and we must realize—that his hope was a distant but necessary dream. As he lamented, the "concept of supremacy is so imbedded in the white society that it will take many years for color to cease to be a judgmental factor." Unless we keep King's sober critique in mind, we will be ineffectual, if not counterproductive, in our efforts to achieve his dream of a genuinely color-blind society.

"The time has come for America to fulfill the promise of equal justice before the law and for the nation to renounce race classifications."

Race Should Not Be a Consideration in Public Policy

Ward Connerly

Ward Connerly is a businessman and a regent of the University of California. He was a leader of the campaign to pass Proposition 209 in California, which in 1997 outlawed racial preferences in all decisions made by the state of California. In the following viewpoint, written in April 2001, Connerly argues that race-based government policies are inherently discriminatory. He points out that the idea that there are separate races has been debunked. Connerly then discusses his sponsorship of California's Racial Privacy Initiative, which would prohibit the state governmnent from classifying individuals by race or ethnicity. The initiative, also known as Proposition 54, was voted down in California's October 2003 election.

As you read, consider the following questions:
1. What two concessions did America's founders make to race, in Connerly's view?
2. What kinds of discriminatory practices did state-based racial classifications help support in the Jim Crow era, in Connerly's opinion?
3. In the author's words, what are some of the reasons that Americans should renounce racial classifications?

Ward Connerly, "Don't Box Me In: An End to Racial Checkoffs," *National Review*, vol. 53, April 16, 2001. Copyright © 2001 by National Review, Inc., 215 Lexington Ave., New York, NY 10016. Reproduced by permission.

A few weeks ago [in April 2001], I was having dinner with a group of supporters following a lecture. One of those in attendance was a delightful woman who applauded my efforts to achieve a colorblind government. She strongly urged me to stay the course, promised financial support for my organization—the American Civil Rights Institute—and proclaimed that what we are doing is best for the nation.

Then, an odd moment occurred, when she said, "What you're doing is also best for your people." I flinched, took a couple of bites of my salad, and gathered my thoughts. I thought: "My people"? Anyone who knows me knows that I abhor this mindset. But this dear lady doesn't know all my views or the nuances of race. She has innocently wandered into a racial thicket and doesn't have a clue that she has just tapped a raw nerve. Do I risk offending her by opening this issue for discussion? Do I risk losing her financial support by evidencing my distaste for what she has said? Perhaps it would be best to ignore the moment and let my staff follow up in pursuit of her support.

I concluded that the situation demanded more of me than to believe that she was incapable of understanding what troubled me about her comment. So, I did what comes naturally in such situations—I politely confronted her. "What did you mean when you referred to 'my people' a moment ago?" I asked. "The black race," she responded. "What is your 'race'?" I asked. She said, "I'm Irish and German." I plowed ahead. "Would it affect your concept of my 'race' if I told you that one of my grandparents was Irish and American Indian, another French Canadian, another of African descent, and the other Irish? Aren't they all 'my people'? What about my children? They consist of my ingredients as well as those of their mother, who is Irish. What about my grandchildren, two of whom have a mother who is half Vietnamese?" The lady was initially awestruck. But that exchange produced one of the richest conversations about race I have ever had.

This discussion is one that an increasing number of Americans are having across our nation. It is one that many more would like to have. Thanks to the race questions placed in the 2000 Census, a great number of people are beginning to wonder about this business of their "race."

Government Should Be Colorblind

From its inception, America has promised equal justice before the law. The Declaration of Independence and the Constitution stand as monuments to the Founders' belief that we can fashion a government of colorblind laws, a unified nation without divisible parts. Unfortunately, they had to compromise on that vision from the beginning. To create a government, they had to protect the international slave trade until 1808. After that time, with the slave trade forever banned, they hoped and believed the slave system would wither away.

In a second concession of their principles to material interests, the Founders also agreed to count slaves as only three-fifths of a person. This compromise stemmed not from a belief that slaves were less than human; rather, slaveowning states wanted to count slaves as whole persons in deciding how large their population was, but not count them at all in deciding how much the states would pay in taxes. The infamous three-fifths compromise was the unfortunate concession.

To distinguish slaves from non-slaves, governments established various race classifications. Unfortunately, these classifications continued long after the Civil War amendments formally repudiated them. After all, once everyone was free to enjoy all the privileges and immunities of American citizenship, there was no longer a need to classify people by race. In hindsight, we recognize that, after nearly a century of race classifications imposed by the state, these classifications had become part of the way average Americans saw themselves, as well as others. Over the next half-century, scientists began to recognize that these race classifications don't exist in nature. We had created them, to justify an inhuman system.

Even as science reached these conclusions, however, these classifications played ever more important roles in American life. Poll taxes and literacy tests; separate bathroom facilities, transportation, water fountains, neighborhoods—the entire Jim Crow system relied on these state-imposed race classifications. And with science unable to distinguish a black person from a non-black person, the government relied on the infamous "one-drop rule": If you have just one drop of "black blood," you're black.

Although the Supreme Court struck down the "separate

The Government's Preoccupation with Race

Scientists today agree that the genetic differences that distinguish members of supposedly different "races" are small, and that the races have become so intermixed that few people can claim to be of racially "pure" origins. The range of biological variation within any one race is far greater than the average differences among races.

And yet the government of the United States, remarkably, still utilizes these antiquated and pernicious categories in compiling statistical information about the American people. The entry on the black population in the index to the 1997 edition of the *Statistical Abstract of the United States* gives 230 citations to tables that distinguish African Americans from other Americans. Another 140 citations direct the reader to data on "Hispanics," a newly invented quasi-racial category. . . . Asians and Pacific Islanders get 42 references, and American Indians and Alaskan natives 47. If you want to know how many African Americans regularly use the Internet, how many Asians were treated in hospital emergency rooms in the preceding year, how many Hispanics usually eat breakfast, or how many American Indians were arrested for burglary, the answers are all there. The federal government inundates us with data that convey the unmistakable message that Americans of different "races" differ from each other in many important ways.

It is very striking that the American public is not bombarded with similar official statistics on the socioeconomic characteristics of Catholics, Protestants, Jews, and Muslims, and the many denominational subdivisions within those broad categories. Why not? . . . Why shouldn't the public be able to find out if Jews are much wealthier than Presbyterians, on the average, or if Mormons are more likely to attend college than Southern Baptists? The government of the United States has never inquired into the religious affiliations of individual citizens because religion is regarded as a private matter in American society and not the business of government. If such information did become readily available, the effect might be to heighten tensions between people of different faiths, inspiring some to complain that they did not have their "fair share" of federal judgeships or of seats on the boards of large corporations and that others were "overrepresented" in those positions.

If not religion, why race?

Stephan Thernstrom, "The Demography of Racial and Ethnic Groups," in Abigail Thernstrom and Stephan Thernstrom, eds., *Beyond the Color Line: New Perspectives on Race and Ethnicity in America*. Stanford, CA: Hoover Institution Press, 2002.

but equal" legal structure, the Court failed to eliminate the race classifications that sustained all the forms of segregation and discrimination the Court was trying to eliminate. We have seen the actual expansion of the groups being classified. On some level, though, I'm sure we really do want to become "one nation . . . indivisible." Witness the tenfold increase in "multiracial" families since 1967. In its decision that year—aptly named *Loving v. Virginia*—the Supreme Court ruled that anti-miscegenation laws (those forbidding people of different races to marry) were unconstitutional. While it took some time for us to shed the taboos against interracial dating and marriage, today there are more "multiracial" children born in California than there are "black" children. When [actors] Benjamin Bratt and Julia Roberts began dating, no one cared that they were an interracial couple. So too with [television personalities] Maury Povich and Connie Chung. Love has become colorblind.

The Racial Privacy Initiative

The time has come for America to fulfill the promise of equal justice before the law and for the nation to renounce race classifications. To that end, I am preparing to place the Racial Privacy Initiative (RPI) before California voters[1]. This initiative would prohibit governments in California from classifying individuals by race, color, ethnicity, or national origin. Much to my surprise, just submitting RPI to the state in preparation for gathering signatures has generated controversy. The American Civil Liberties Union has called it a "racist" initiative, and various proponents of race preferences have said it will "turn back the clock on civil rights."

In drafting RPI, we have exempted medical research and have proposed nothing that would prevent law-enforcement officers from identifying particular individuals, so long as those methods are already lawful. To guarantee that laws against discrimination are enforced, we have exempted the Department of Fair Employment and Housing from the provisions of RPI for ten years.

Getting the government out of the business of classifying

1. RPI was voted down in California's 2003 election.

its citizens and asking them to check these silly little race boxes represents the next step in our nation's long journey toward becoming one nation. Getting rid of these boxes will strike a blow against the overbearing race industry that has grown like Topsy in America. It will help free us from the costly and poisonous identity politics and the racial spoils system that define our political process. It will clip the wings of a government that has become so intrusive that it classifies its citizens on the basis of race, even when citizens "decline to state." Enacting the Racial Privacy Initiative is the most significant step we can take to bring Americans together.

I ask all Americans who share the goal of a united America to join in this endeavor to fulfill our Founders' promise of colorblind justice before the law. For my part, I just don't want to be boxed in.

"A large debt is owed by America to the descendants of America's slaves."

The U.S. Government Should Pay Reparations to Blacks for Slavery

Randall Robinson

Randall Robinson is the author of *The Debt: What America Owes to Blacks*. In the following viewpoint he argues that the U.S. government should pay reparations to the descendants of slaves. Slavery, he contends, is responsible for the current wealth gap between blacks and whites in America, and reparations would be a major step toward resolving this racial inequality. Moreover, he argues, the United States has a moral obligation to make amends for the centuries-long crime of slavery.

As you read, consider the following questions:
1. Why did Reconstructionist legislation providing reparations to slaves fail, according to Robinson?
2. How does Robinson define "contemporaneousness"?
3. How will making a case for reparations benefit the spirit of African Americans, in the author's view?

Randall Robinson, "Reparations—More than Just a Check," *The Black Collegian*, vol. 33, February 2003. Copyright © 2003 by iMinorities, Inc. Reproduced by permission.

In the wonderful book *Strong Men Keep Coming* by Tonya Bolden, there is a reprint of a letter dated August 7, 1865, written by Jourdon Anderson, who was once a slave in Big Spring, Tennessee. The letter is written to his former owner, Colonel P.H. Anderson, who had written to the ex-slave in Dayton, Ohio, where he had resettled with his wife and children. The colonel had written to persuade Anderson to return to Big Spring and work for him as a free man.

Sir:

I got your letter, and was glad to find that you had not forgotten Jourdan, and that you wanted me to come back and live with you again, promising to do better for me than anybody else can. . . .

I want to know particularly what the good chance is you propose to give me. I am doing tolerably well here. I get twenty-five dollars a month, with victuals and clothing; have a comfortable home for Mandy,—the folks call her Mrs. Anderson, —and the children—Milly Jane and Grundy—go to school and are learning well. . . . Now if you will write and say what wages you will give me, I will be better able to decide whether it would be to my advantage to move back again.

As to my freedom, which you say I can have, there is nothing to be gained on that score, as I got my freedom papers in 1864 from the Provost-Marshall-General of the Department of Nashville. Mandy says she would be afraid to go back without some proof that you were disposed to treat us justly and kindly; and we have concluded to test your sincerity by asking you to send us our wages for the time we served you.

I served you faithfully for thirty-two years, and Mandy twenty-years. At twenty-five dollars a month for me, two dollars a week for Mandy, our earnings would amount [to] eleven thousand six hundred and eighty dollars. Add to the interest for the time our wages have been kept back, deduct what you paid for our clothing, and three doctor's visits for me, and pulling a tooth for Mandy, and the balance will show what we are in justice entitled to. . . .

Please send the money by Adam's Express, in care of V. Winters, Esq., Dayton, Ohio. If you fail to pay us for our faithful labors in the past, we can have little faith in your promises in the future. We trust the good Maker has opened your eyes to the wrongs which you and your fathers have done to me and my fathers, in making us toil for you for generations without recompense. . . . Surely there will be a day of reckoning for those who defraud the laborer of his hire. . . .

Say howdy to George Carter, and thank him for taking the pistol from you when you were shooting at me.

Colonel Anderson never paid Jourdon Anderson what was owed him for his labor, nor had any of the other slaveholders (including George Washington and Thomas Jefferson) who had stolen the labor of tens of millions of blacks and, by so doing, robbed the futures of all who would descend from them. And the United States government was complicit in this mass injustice of defrauding "the laborer of his hire."

Precedents for Reparations

Following emancipation, former slaves began asserting that they be paid the debt owed them if "emancipation" was to be more than a legal technicality. Indeed, both the U.S. House of Representatives and the U.S. Senate passed legislation providing reparations to America's former slaves. President Andrew Johnson, a pre-emancipation slaveholder, vetoed the legislation, however.

With black Americans continuing to press for their own reparations, David Ben-Gurion responded thusly to Jews being awarded reparations by post-war Germany via the 1952 Luxembourg Agreement:

> . . . a precedent has been created by which a great State, as a result of moral pressure alone, takes it upon itself to pay compensation to the victims of the government that preceded it. For the first time in the history [of an] era [where people have] been persecuted, oppressed, plundered and despoiled for hundreds of years in the countries of Europe, a persecutor and despoiler has been obliged to return part of his spoils and has even undertaken to make collective reparation as partial compensation for material losses.

Some would argue that such an obligation does not obtain in the case of the black holocaust because the wrongful action took place so long ago. Such arguments are specious at best. Indeed, in 1994, seventy-one years after the Rosewood massacre in which white lynch mobs killed blacks and drove survivors into the swamps near a prosperous black community in Florida, Governor Lawton Chiles signed into law a bill (House Bill 591) that provided for the payment of $2.1 million in reparations to the descendants of the black victims of Rosewood.

In addition, slavery did not really end in 1865, as is commonly believed, but was extended well into the twentieth century. As Yuval Taylor has pointed out in *I Was Born a Slave:*

Although it was no longer called slavery, the post-Reconstruction Southern practices of peonage, forced convict labor, and to a lesser degree sharecropping essentially continued the institution of slavery well into the twentieth century, and were in some ways even worse. (Peonage, for example, was a complex system in which a black man would be arrested for "vagrancy," another word for unemployment, ordered to pay a fine he could not afford and incarcerated. A plantation owner would pay his fine and "hire" him until he could afford to pay off the fine himself: The peon was then forced to work locked up at night, and, if he ran away, chased by bloodhounds until recaptured. One important difference between peonage and slavery was that while slaves had considerable monetary value for the plantation owner; peons had almost none, and could therefore be mistreated—and even murdered—without monetary loss.

Slavery and Modern Racial Inequality

What slavery had firmly established in the way of debilitating psychic pain and a lopsidedly unequal economic relationship of blacks to whites, formal organs of state and federal government would cement in law for the century that followed. Thus it should surprise no one that the wealth gap (wealth defined as the net value of assets) separating blacks from whites over the twentieth century has mushroomed beyond any ability of black earned income ever to close it. This too is the fruit of long-term structural racial discrimination, government sponsored in many cases, acquiesced to in others.

So you can see that an unbroken story line of evidence and logic drawn across time from Jamestown to Appomattox to contemporary America renders the "it's too late" response to reparations for African Americans inadequate. For blacks, the destructive moral crime that began in Jamestown in 1619 has yet to end.

Well before the birth of our country, Europe and the eventual United States perpetrated a heinous wrong against the peoples of Africa—and sustained and benefited from the wrong for centuries. In 1965, after nearly 350 years of legal racial suppression, the United States enacted the Voting

Rights Act and, virtually simultaneously, began to walk away from the social wreckage that centuries of white hegemony had wrought. The country then began to rub itself with the memory-emptying salve of contemporaneousness. (If the wrong did not just occur, then the living cannot be deemed in any way responsible.)

An Honest Dialogue

I believe . . . that the greatest and most lasting benefit of the national reparations debate will be to foster an honest discussion about the historical consequences and moral challenges presented by structural racism. The reparations debate reflects the central conflict over the nature of U.S. democracy and the possibilities of transformation for a deep racialized and class-stratified society. From the vantage point of those favoring black reparations, racial peace can come about only as a product of social justice—coming to terms with the meaning of American, and even Western, civilization, as they have structured the unequal realities of life for millions of people of African descent. As historian and Garvey scholar Robert Hill observed in a conversation about the issue, the campaign for black reparations is "the final chapter in the five hundred year struggle to suppress the transatlantic slave trade, slavery, and the consequences of its effects."

Manning Marable, *The Great Walls of Democracy: The Meaning of Race in American Life*. New York: BasicCivitas Books, 2002.

But when the black living suffer real and current consequences as a result of wrongs committed by a younger America, then contemporary America must be caused to shoulder responsibility for those wrongs until such wrongs have been adequately compensated and righted. The life and responsibilities of a society or nation are not circumscribed by the life spans of its mortal constituents. Social rights, wrongs, obligations, and responsibilities flow eternal.

American capitalism, which starts each child where its parents left off, is not a fair system. This is particularly the case for African Americans, whose general economic starting points have been rearmost in our society because of slavery and its long racialist aftermath. American slaves for two and a half centuries saw taken from them the economic value of their labor which, were it a line item in today's gross national product report, would undoubtedly run into the hundreds of billions of dollars. Whether the monetary obligation is legally enforceable or not, therefore, a large debt is owed by America to the descendants of America's slaves.

Remembering the Past

Here, habit has become our enemy, for America has made an art form by now of grinding its past deeds, no matter how despicable, into mere ephemera. African Americans unfortunately, have accommodated this habit of American amnesia all too well. It would behoove African Americans to remember that history forgets, first, those who forget themselves. To do what is necessary to accomplish anything approaching psychic and economic parity in the next half century will not only require a fundamental attitude shift in American thinking, but massive amounts of money as well. Before the country in general can be made to understand, African Americans themselves must come to understand that this demand is not for charity. It is simply for what they are owed on a debt that is old but compellingly obvious and valid still.

Even the making of a well-reasoned case for restitution will do wonders for the spirit of African Americans. It will cause them at long last to understand the genesis of their dilemma by gathering, as have all other groups, all of their history—before, during, and after slavery—into one story of themselves. To hold the story fast to their breast. To make of it, over time, a sacred text. And from it, to explain themselves to themselves and to their heirs. Tall again, as they had been long, long ago.

"It is well past time for Blacks to concede that they are indeed American and that this country, in numerous ways, has admitted its past injustices to us."

The U.S. Government Should Not Pay Reparations to Blacks for Slavery

E.R. Shipp

E.R. Shipp is a columnist for the *New York Daily News*. In the following viewpoint he argues that the reparations-for-slavery movement is misguided and motivated in large part by an "us-them" mentality that has a divisive effect on race relations. Shipp maintains that the United States has taken heed of the debt it owes for slavery, in the form of social welfare programs dating back to the 1960s, affirmative action policies, a formal apology for slavery from President Bill Clinton in 1998, and ongoing efforts to alleviate urban poverty. Rather than viewing themselves as victims of slavery, Shipp believes that blacks should join the rest of America in confronting social problems as one people.

As you read, consider the following questions:

1. Why are blacks not in the same category as Japanese Americans who received compensation for their internment during World War II, in Shipp's view?
2. What blacks does Shipp view as particularly undeserving of slavery reparations?
3. What issues does the author claim should be addressed by all Americans?

E.R. Shipp, "Does America Owe Us?" *Essence*, vol. 33, February 2003. Copyright © 2003 by Essence Communications, Inc. Reproduced by permission of the author.

The least-remembered portion of Dr. Martin Luther King, Jr.'s speech at the 1963 March on Washington was this passage:

> When the architects of our republic wrote the magnificent words of the Constitution and the Declaration of Independence, they were signing a promissory note to which every American was to fall heir. This note was a promise that all men would be guaranteed the inalienable rights of life, liberty and the pursuit of happiness. It is obvious today that America has defaulted on this promissory note insofar as her citizens of color are concerned. Instead of honoring this sacred obligation, America has given the Negro people a bad check, which has come back marked "insufficient funds." But we refuse to believe that the bank of justice is bankrupt. We refuse to believe that there are insufficient funds in the great vaults of opportunity of this nation.

"They Owe Us!"

And I, for one, refuse to believe that nothing has changed since 1963, that America has not honored, or begun to honor, that promissory note. Unfortunately, too many Black Americans today, often egged on by politicians and preachers and professors who don't mind dazzling their audiences with sound-good inanities and foolishness, are running around hollering, "They owe us!" Mind you, they are a minority among us so-called minorities. Exhibit A: Only three or four thousand people showed up in Washington in August [2002] for what had been billed as the Millions for Reparations March.

Some members of this movement, no doubt looking at their bank accounts or reflecting on the difficulties they are experiencing in these tough economic times, are salivating at the thought of a paycheck, even if they cannot identify a single slave from their past. Others are so desperate for excuses to explain their own failures, so embittered and so jealous of White people that they go through life feeling what a New York City councilman, Charles Barron, said at the reparations march: "I want to go up to the closest White person and say, 'You can't understand this; it's a Black thing' and then slap him, just for my mental health."

These are the people who proclaim, "They owe us!" when

Poisoning Race Relations

The U.S. already made a mighty payment for the sin of slavery. It was called the Civil War. . . .

In all, more than 620,000 Americans died in the struggle to eliminate slavery. That is more than the number killed in all of our other wars combined. It amounted to a staggering 1.8 percent of our total population in 1865. That would be the equivalent of killing more than 5 million young Americans today.

Our nation surely did run up a "debt" (as reparations advocates like Randall Robinson . . . like to put it) for allowing black bondage. But that bill was finally paid off, in blood.

And not only in blood. After tardily recognizing their error, Americans have tried to compensate for the historic harm visited upon African Americans. The massive infusions of money into income support, education, and special programs to benefit blacks that activists like Robinson are now calling for have already been offered up. Economist Walter Williams notes that over the last generation the American people have particularly targeted the black underclass with more than $6.1 trillion in anti-poverty spending. . . .

But to the activists, this is not nearly enough. Perhaps there can never be enough done to placate them, because many are driven by an implacable sense of grievance more than a practical desire to see blacks flourish. In his book *The Debt*, Randall Robinson insists that blacks do not like America, and cannot be part of it. It's clear that is his own posture, and he actively urges other African Americans to share it. "*You are owed*" he tells his audience. "*They did this to you*" (with the italic emphasis in his text).

This is a poisonous political path. It will be psychologically unhealthy for many blacks, and it is very likely to inspire a nasty blacklash among other Americans.

Karl Zinsmeister, *American Enterprise*, July 2001.

---

the antecedents for those pronouns are profoundly confusing. I am—proudly—part of "they" if "they" means Americans who have given blood, sweat and tears for this country. I am a "they" who can trace my past back to slaves of African and Native American and European descent in Georgia and North Carolina and to their progeny, who spread throughout the country during slavery and after. I am a "they" whose family has been involved, in one way or another, in every war since the first one that mattered, the Revolutionary War. I give quarter to no one who would deny me the right to be counted among the "theys."

I am an "us" in the view of the reparationists only because I am Black. And that, for them, is all that matters. But what about those Blacks whose ancestors may have been enslaved not in North Carolina or Georgia, but in Jamaica or Haiti? Why should the American government compensate them for what the British or the Spanish or the French might have done? And what about Black Africans in this country? Do they file claims on the basis of some putative connection to a Kunta Kinte in their family tree?

America Has Acknowledged Its Debt to Blacks

It is well past time for Blacks to concede that they are indeed American and that this country, in numerous ways, has admitted its past injustices to us. From the abolitionist movements of the eighteenth and nineteenth centuries to President Johnson's Great Society of the 1960's, this country has taken heed of its debt to Blacks—as well as its debt to others who have been mistreated, tossed aside, left behind. In planning a policy that became affirmative action during the Nixon years, LBJ, a Texan, acknowledged in 1965 "the devastating heritage of long years of slavery and a century of oppression, hatred and injustice." Years later, President Bill Clinton apologized for slavery during his precedent-setting visit to the African continent. No credible history curriculum would dare ignore the Black part of the U.S. story.

Blacks as a whole are not in the same category as Jews who received compensation from the German government, or Japanese-Americans who received compensation from the U.S. government. Those groups received reparations for specific acts of injustice that they, not their ancestors, suffered. Where Blacks have such clearly defined grievances . . . they have the legitimate right to demand compensation. The rest of us should just get over it and move on, realizing that we are much better off for being part of the "they"—Americans—than we would be had our ancestors never left Africa.

The truth is that Blacks suffer little that other Americans don't also suffer. The "debt," which this nation began paying with such acts as the establishment of [historically black]

Howard University in 1867, is being paid in every act of government or the civic sector that tries to eliminate poverty, improve failing school systems, make affordable housing available, provide job training, or pave the way for health-care insurance. Rather than wasting time on this ridiculous reparations movement, we'd be better off joining forces with other Americans to resolve the issues that affect us all.

Periodical Bibliography

The following articles have been selected to supplement the diverse views presented in this chapter.

Pamela Burdman — "Connerly Initiative Would Ban Collection of Racial Data," *Black Issues in Higher Education*, June 20, 2002.

Danny Duncan Collum — "Color Lines and Party Lines: Race and Politics in 2004," *Sojourners*, August 2004.

Ellis Cose — "Discharging a Debt," *Black Enterprise*, July 2004.

Edward J. Erler — "Is the Constitution Color-Blind?" *USA Today*, July 2004.

Nathan Glazer — "Do We Need the Census Race Question?" *Public Interest*, Fall 2002.

John Leo — "Enslaved to the Past," *U.S. News & World Report*, April 15, 2002.

Deroy Murdock — "Connerly Leads Fight to Establish Color-Blind Society," *Insight on the News*, July 1, 2002.

Deroy Murdock — "Should the U.S. Pay Reparations for Slavery? In a Word: No," *Vital Speeches of the Day*, April 15, 2002.

New American — "Slavery Reparations . . . to Whom?" April 19, 2004.

Newsweek — "Debating the Wages of Slavery," August 27, 2001.

Joseph C. Phillips — "Why Don't We Want What We Fought For?" *Newsweek*, April 8, 2002.

Jonathan Rauch — "Blacks Deserve Reparations—but Not for Slavery," *National Journal*, September 1, 2001.

Debra Rosenberg — "Not Just Black and White," *Newsweek*, June 30, 2003.

Rachel Hartigan Shea — "What's the Place of Race?" *U.S. News & World Report*, March 31, 2003.

Carol M. Swain — "Race and Representation," *American Prospect*, June 2004.

Megan Twohey — "Promise Unrealized," *National Journal*, December 16, 2000.

CHAPTER 4

How Can Society Improve Race Relations?

Chapter Preface

The debate over racial issues often focuses on national trends and federal initiatives, but many efforts to improve race relations often happen at the local level. Increasingly, communities, businesses, and schools are using diversity training to address the issue of race relations. Diversity training can take many forms, but the most common is a seminar or workshop in which participants are encouraged to discuss their personal experiences with racism. The overall goal is to encourage participants to deal with cultural and racial differences more sensitively. Diversity training has become a multimillion-dollar industry, with dozens of companies and hundreds of individual consultants offering training sessions. Some are nonprofit or charge only a nominal fee to local schools or community organizations, while those catering to corporate clients may receive more than $5,000 a day. Certificate programs in diversity training are now being offered by some colleges and online educators. The trend also has spawned a magazine, *Managing Diversity*, and dozens of books.

Diversity training has its share of critics, both conservative and liberal. Some conservatives view diversity training as ineffective and merely a way for businesses and other organizations to appear "politically correct." Many liberals, on the other hand, worry that in focusing on the racial tensions among specific members of a group, diversity training ignores the broader problem of structural racism. History professor Elisabeth Lasch-Quinn makes this argument in her book *Race Experts: How Racial Etiquette, Sensitivity Training, and New Age Therapy Hijacked the Civil Rights Revolution*. Write journalists Daisy Hernandez and Kendra Field in *Colorlines Magazine*, "Whether the diversity industry exploits racial problems without advancing substantive change is still a relevant question, especially as the industry's influence spreads."

While it may not be perfect, supporters of diversity training argue, the popularity of such programs is a sign that organizations have made improving race relations a priority. The authors in the following chapter examine other ways that individuals, businesses, and schools can improve race relations.

"What, when each generation is more racially and ethnically mixed than its predecessor, does race even mean anymore?"

Interracial Marriages Will Lead to Greater Racial Harmony

Gregory Rodriguez

Gregory Rodriguez is a senior fellow at the New America Foundation and a contributing editor of the *Los Angeles Times* opinion section. In the following viewpoint he argues that interracial marriages—and the multiracial children they produce—are slowly transforming Americans' traditional, over-simplified views about race. Rates of interracial marriage are rising, he writes, and as they continue to do so, more and more Americans will identify with multiple races. Rodriguez notes that rates of intermarriage are highest among Latinos, and he argues that the United States is beginning to embrace the Mexican celebration of racial and cultural synthesis. Rodriguez believes that race relations in America will be transformed not by government policy but by cultural trends such as intermarriage.

As you read, consider the following questions:

1. What percentage of African Americans will claim mixed ancestry by 2100, according to Rodriguez?
2. What two groups are most open to intermarriage, according to the author?
3. What is the pre–civil rights "one-drop" rule, as explained by Rodriguez?

Gregory Rodriguez, "Mongrel America," *Atlantic Monthly*, vol. 291, January/February 2003. Copyright © 2003 by The Atlantic Monthly Group. Reproduced by permission of the author.

Are racial categories still an important—or even a valid—tool of government policy? In recent years the debate in America has been between those who think that race is paramount and those who think it is increasingly irrelevant, and in the next election cycle this debate will surely intensify around a California ballot initiative that would all but prohibit the state from asking its citizens what their racial backgrounds are. But the ensuing polemics will only obscure the more fundamental question: What, when each generation is more racially and ethnically mixed than its predecessor, does race even mean anymore? If your mother is Asian and your father is African-American, what, racially speaking, are you? (And if your spouse is half Mexican and half Russian Jewish, what are your children?)

Intermarriage and Mixed Ancestry

Five decades after the end of legal segregation, and only thirty-six years after the Supreme Court struck down anti-miscegenation laws, young African-Americans are considerably more likely than their elders to claim mixed heritage. A study by the Population Research Center, in Portland, Oregon, projects that the black intermarriage rate will climb dramatically in this century, to a point at which 37 percent of African-Americans will claim mixed ancestry by 2100. By then more than 40 percent of Asian-Americans will be mixed. Most remarkable, however, by century's end the number of Latinos claiming mixed ancestry will be more than two times the number claiming a single background.

Not surprisingly, intermarriage rates for all groups are highest in the states that serve as immigration gateways. By 1990 Los Angeles County had an intermarriage rate five times the national average. Latinos and Asians, the groups that have made up three quarters of immigrants over the past forty years, have helped to create a climate in which ethnic or racial intermarriage is more accepted today than ever before. Nationally, whereas only eight percent of foreign-born Latinos marry non-Latinos, 32 percent of second-generation and 57 percent of third-generation Latinos marry outside their ethnic group. Similarly, whereas only 13 percent of foreign-born Asians marry non-Asians, 34 percent of second-generation and 54 percent of third-generation Asian-Americans do.

Meanwhile, as everyone knows, Latinos are now the largest minority group in the nation. Two thirds of Latinos, in turn, are of Mexican heritage. This is significant in itself, because their sheer numbers have helped Mexican-Americans do more than any other group to alter the country's old racial thinking. For instance, Texas and California, where Mexican-Americans are the largest minority, were the first two states to abolish affirmative action: when the collective "minority" populations in those states began to outnumber whites, the racial balance that had made affirmative action politically viable was subverted.

Many Mexican-Americans now live in cities or regions where they are a majority, changing the very idea of what it means to be a member of a "minority" group. Because of such demographic changes, a number of the policies designed to integrate non-whites into the mainstream—affirmative action in college admissions, racial set-asides in government contracting—have been rendered more complicated or even counterproductive in recent years. In California cities where whites have become a minority, it is no longer clear what "diversity" means or what the goals of integration policies should be. The selective magnet-school program of the Los Angeles Unified School District, for example, was originally developed as an alternative to forced busing—a way to integrate ethnic-minority students by encouraging them to look beyond their neighborhoods. Today, however, the school district is 71 percent Latino, and Latinos' majority status actually puts them at a disadvantage when applying to magnet schools.

Mestizaje

But it is not merely their growing numbers (they will soon be the majority in both California and Texas, and they are already the single largest contemporary immigrant group nationwide) that make Mexican-Americans a leading indicator of the country's racial future; rather, it's what they represent. They have always been a complicating element in the American racial system, which depends on an oversimplified classification scheme. Under the pre-civil-rights formulation, for example, if you had "one drop" of African blood, you were

Racial Composition of the United States According to the 2000 Census

Race	Number	% of Total Population
Single Race Only	*274,595,678*	*97.57*
White	211,460,626	75.14
Black or African American	34,652,190	12.32
American Indian and Alaska Native	2,475,956	0.88
Asian	10,242,998	3.64
Native Hawaiian and other Pacific Islander	398,835	0.14
Some other race	15,359,073	5.46
Two Races	*6,368,075*	*2.26*
White and black	784,764	0.28
White and American Indian	1,082,683	0.38
White and Asian	868,395	0.31
White and Native American	112,964	0.04
White and some other race	2,206,251	0.78
Black and American Indian	182,494	0.06
Black and Asian	106,782	0.04
Black and Native American	29,786	0.01
Black and some other race	417,249	0.15
American Indian and Asian	52,429	0.02
American Indian and Native Hawaiian	7,328	0.00
American Indian and some other race	93,842	0.03
Asian and Native Hawaiian	138,802	0.05
Asian and some other race	249,108	0.09
Native Hawaiian and some other race	35,108	0.01
Three or More Races	*458,153*	*0.16*
Total	281,421,906	100.00

U.S. Census Bureau (2001). *Population by Race and Hispanic or Latino Origin for the United States: 1990 and 2000 (PHC-T-1). Tables 1 and 2.*

fully black. The scheme couldn't accommodate people who were part one thing and part another. Mexicans, who are a product of intermingling—both cultural and genetic—between the Spanish and the many indigenous peoples of North and Central America, have a history of tolerating and even reveling in such ambiguity. Since the conquest of Mexico, in the sixteenth century, they have practiced *mestizaje*—racial and cultural synthesis—both in their own country and as they came north. Unlike the English-speaking settlers of the western frontier, the Spaniards were willing everywhere they went to allow racial and cultural mixing to blur the lines between themselves and the natives. The fact that Latin America is far more heavily populated by people of mixed ancestry than Anglo America is the clearest sign of the difference between the two outlooks on race.

Nativists once deplored the Mexican tendency toward hybridity. In the mid nineteenth century, at the time of the conquest of the Southwest, Secretary of State James Buchanan feared granting citizenship to a "mongrel race." And in the late 1920s Representative John C. Box, of Texas, warned his colleagues on the House Immigration and Naturalization Committee that the continued influx of Mexican immigrants could lead to the "distressing process of mongrelization" in America. He argued that because Mexicans were the products of mixing, they harbored a relaxed attitude toward interracial unions and were likely to mingle freely with other races in the United States.

Box was right. The typical cultural isolation of immigrants notwithstanding, those immigrants' children and grandchildren are strongly oriented toward the American melting pot. Today two thirds of multiracial and multiethnic births in California involve a Latino parent. Mexicanidad, or "Mexicanness," is becoming the catalyst for a new American cultural synthesis.

Beyond Black and White

In the same way that the rise in the number of multiracial Americans muddles U.S. racial statistics, the growth of the Mexican-American mestizo population has begun to challenge the Anglo-American binary view of race. In the 1920 census Mexicans were counted as whites. Ten years later they were reassigned to a separate Mexican "racial" category. In 1940 they were officially reclassified as white. Today almost half the Latinos in California, which is home to a third of the nation's Latinos (most of them of Mexican descent), check "other" as their race. In the first half of the twentieth century Mexican-American advocates fought hard for the privileges that came with being white in America. But since the 1960s activists have sought to reap the benefits of being nonwhite minorities. Having spent so long trying to fit into one side or the other of the binary system, Mexican-Americans have become numerous and confident enough to simply claim their brownness—their mixture. This is a harbinger of America's future.

The original melting-pot concept was incomplete: it applied only to white ethnics (Irish, Italians, Poles, and so forth), not to blacks and other nonwhites. Israel Zangwill, the playwright whose 1908 drama *The Melting Pot* popularized the concept, even wrote that whites were justified in avoiding intermarriage with blacks. In fact, multiculturalism—the ideology that promotes the permanent coexistence of separate but equal cultures in one place—can be seen as a by-product of America's exclusion of African-Americans from the melting pot; those whom assimilation rejected came to reject assimilation. Although the multicultural movement has always encompassed other groups, blacks gave it its moral impetus.

A New American Identity

But the immigrants of recent decades are helping to forge a new American identity, something more complex than either a melting pot or a confederation of separate but equal groups. And this identity is emerging not as a result of politics or any specific public policies but because of powerful underlying cultural forces. To be sure, the civil-rights movement was instrumental in the initial assault on racial barriers. And immigration policies since 1965 have tended to favor those immigrant groups—Asians and Latinos—who are most open to intermarriage. But in recent years the government's major contribution to the country's growing multiracialism has been—as it should continue to be—a retreat from dictating limits on interracial intimacy and from exalting (through such policies as racial set-asides and affirmative action) race as the most important American category of being. As a result, Americans cross racial lines more often than ever before in choosing whom to sleep with, marry, or raise children with.

Unlike the advances of the civil-rights movement, the future of racial identity in America is unlikely to be determined by politics or the courts or public policy. Indeed, at this point perhaps the best thing the government can do is to acknowledge changes in the meaning of race in America and then get out of the way. The Census Bureau's decision to allow Americans to check more than one box in the "race" section of the 2000 Census was an important step in this direction. No longer forced to choose a single racial identity, Americans are now free to identify themselves as mestizos—and with this newfound freedom we may begin to endow racial issues with the complexity and nuance they deserve.

"As appealing as the discourse celebrating interracial love might be, it ignores the continued salience of race in American society."

The Effect of Interracial Marriages on Race Relations Is Exaggerated

Renee C. Romano

Renee C. Romano is a professor of history and African American studies at Wesleyan University and the author of *Race Mixing: Black-White Marriage in Postwar America*, from which the following viewpoint is excerpted. In it, she rejects the idea that interracial marriage is a major part of the solution to America's racial problems. She notes that black-white marriages are still rare. Moreover, she argues that the focus on intermarriage and individuals' views toward it obscures the broader problem of institutional racism, which Romano believes is deeply entrenched in U.S. society. In her view U.S. society will not truly be integrated—and intermarriages will not truly become widespread—until there are no longer clear disadvantages associated with being black.

As you read, consider the following questions:

1. Approximately how many black-white marriages are there in America, according to the author?
2. What does Dinesh D'Souza hope will be the result of increasing numbers of multiracial children?
3. In Romano's opinion, what is the most important factor limiting the rate of black-white intermarriage?

In March 1977 in Middletown, Connecticut, the short-lived Interracial Clubs of America founded a new magazine that advocated interracial marriage as the solution to America's race problems. *Interracial* was dedicated "to the proposition of developing a totally integrated America through intermarriage." Interracial marriages not only would bring people of different racial and ethnic backgrounds together, but would also produce biracial children who could transcend America's historical racial divide. Individuals who married interracially could achieve what the legal reforms of the civil rights movement had failed to do, *Interracial* asserted. Its motto explained, "Love is the answer, not legislation."

Is Love Really the Answer?

Today politicians, the media, and popular culture commonly describe cross-racial love as a positive good that will help reduce racial animosity. In 1998 the *Washington Post* argued that then defense secretary William Cohen's marriage to a black woman was "the best advertisement for the kind of dialogue and interpersonal racial progress President Bill Clinton is now pushing, the kind of progress that can't be legislated." Warren Beatty's 1998 political satire, *Bulworth*, preached a similar message about the importance of interracial relationships in overcoming America's racist history. In *Bulworth*, Beatty plays a disillusioned American senator who takes on a role as truth-teller during a reelection campaign. Soon he's wearing hip-hop clothes, rapping his message, and courting a black woman half his age. Near the end of the film, Bulworth announces to a crowd of supporters that the only way to end racism is through widespread interracial sex, for "everyone to f— everyone else." All we need to achieve racial harmony, the senator raps on national TV, is "a voluntary, free-spirited, open-ended program of procreative racial deconstruction." When asked in an interview about the movie why he had decided to advocate interracial sex as the solution to the race problem, Beatty replied, "If you're doing a movie about race and you want to offer any kind of conclusive suggestion, that would be it. It's called love."

Interracial love in these accounts is an, or even *the*, answer to how to improve American race relations. Proponents of this idea cite a variety of reasons why love and marriage across the color line have the potential to undo racial hierarchies. Some focus on the importance of multiracial children, whose very existence not only will undermine racial categories, but who also may have a unique ability to serve as racial ambassadors, shuttling back and forth between each of their racial homes in an effort to make peace. As one biracial man argued recently, multiracial people are "uniquely positioned to be sensitive, objective negotiators of intergroup conflict." Others argue that interracial relationships will serve as a mechanism for the transfer of wealth from whites to nonwhites, that these relationships will lead a growing number of intermarried whites and their relatives to redraw their map of "racial self-interest" to include blacks, or that intermarried whites can best educate other whites about the damage caused by racism. Interracial marriage will thus produce a set of whites whose interest in racial justice will be more immediate and lasting than that of "white liberals who happen to live in the suburbs." According to the legal scholar Randall Kennedy, "few situations are more likely to mobilize the racially privileged individual to move against racial wrongs than witnessing such wrongs inflicted upon one's mother-in-law, father-in-law, spouse or child." Family ties across racial lines, another legal scholar argues, "will more quickly consume racial animus than any other social or legal force."

Yet given the still small numbers of black-white marriages, even if these marriages do serve as a meaningful method of wealth transmission or lead some whites to become blacks' racial allies, their influence will be quite limited. With less than four hundred thousand black-white couples in contemporary America, only a very small minority of blacks will receive any economic benefit from intermarriage. Even if all intermarried whites became crusaders for racial justice, they would still represent only a tiny percentage of whites overall. . . .

Ignoring Institutional Racism

The "love is the answer" discourse implies that whites' willingness to accept blacks as their social equals will automatically lead to meaningful racial equality in the United States. Yet racial inequalities today are primarily structural and institutional, rather than the result of individual racist acts or attitudes. Despite the gains of the civil rights movement and the growth of a sizable black middle class, structural racial inequality remains embedded in American politics and institutions. One of every two black children today lives below the poverty line; four times as many black families as white live in poverty; black unemployment rates are two to three times that of whites. Racial minorities are far more likely than whites to live near toxic waste dumps, to be arrested on drug charges, and to be denied mortgage loans. Blacks are far more likely than Asians or Latinos to live in segregated neighborhoods, no matter what their income level. Blacks live, on average, in neighborhoods that are 60 percent black. The level of segregation in the public schools remains high

Census Figures on Intermarriage

Number of Married Couples (in thousands) and Percent of Married Couples by Race and Hispanic Origin

	Number (thousands)	Percent
Married Couples	56,497	100%
Race		
Same Race Couples	55,029	97.4
Both White	48,917	86.6
Both Black	3,989	7.1
Both Asian	1,914	3.4
Both Other Race	209	0.4
Interracial Couples	1,047	1.9
Black/White	363	0.06
Black/Asian	25	0.04
White/Asian	655	1.2
Other Combinations	4	0.01
Hispanic Origin		
Both Hispanic	4,739	8.4
Both Non-Hispanic	50,015	88.5
Hispanic/Non-Hispanic	1,743	3.1

Jason Fields and Lynne M. Casper, 2001, America's Families and Living Arrangements, 2000. Current Population Reports, P20-537. U.S. Census Bureau, Washington, DC.

despite the *Brown* ruling prohibiting segregation in public education. In 1980 nearly one-third of black students attended all-minority schools, and three out of five attended schools that were predominantly black. School segregation today is due more to residential patterns than to laws, but it remains a fact of life for most young blacks and whites. . . .

As appealing as the discourse celebrating interracial love might be, it ignores the continued salience of race in American society. Focusing on the acts of individual blacks and whites simplifies complex problems and contributes to the removal of racial issues from the public sphere. As the critical legal race theorist Patricia Williams asserts, suggesting intermarriage as the way to end racial inequality in American society is a "romantic solution posing as a political tool." This discourse further reinforces the belief that racism is the work of isolated racists rather than something systemic or structural. The notion that "love is the answer" serves to mask existing inequalities, not to undo remaining racial hierarchies.

The Conservative Spin on Intermarriage

Tellingly, this idea has been embraced most emphatically by those on the right who oppose affirmative action programs, believe "identity politics" are balkanizing the nation, and contend that ongoing racial divisions are the artificial creation of a liberal elite. At the core of these writers' arguments is the assertion that rising approval for interracial dating and marriage proves that white racism is no longer a serious problem that limits opportunities for blacks, and thus government-sponsored remedies to benefit blacks are no longer needed. Intermarriage rates are used to discredit pundits and social scientists who insist that high incarceration rates for black males, continuing income inequalities between blacks and whites, and high black poverty rates mean that blacks remain disadvantaged in American society. The historian Stephan Thernstrom thus questioned a pessimistic 1998 report on race that called for government initiatives to aid the inner-city poor and to reform the American criminal justice system by pointing to evidence of better interpersonal relations between blacks and whites: "If you look at social contact, it is increased markedly. Interracial dating is up. Interracial marriage, the same. Whatever the fault lines are in our society, the idea that it is the old-fashioned black and white seems to me fairly simplistic."

Rising intermarriage rates, furthermore, are thought to ensure that government programs aimed at racial redress are no longer necessary. Dinesh D'Souza, a political pundit whose book *The End of Racism* argues that existing racial inequality is due to a deficient black culture, thus looks forward to the day when the increasing number of multiracial children will make it impossible for the government to sort people into categories for the purpose of enforcing affirmative action policies. Calling race-entitlement programs "pure political pork" supported by civil rights activists who have rejected the color-blind principles of predecessors such as Martin Luther King, Jr., and Frederick Douglass, D'Souza celebrates the growing number of multiracial children who are "literally beyond racial classification." This emerging American "café au lait society" will soon mean that the government will be unable to count citizens by race, D'Souza predicts, and thus everything from college admissions to hiring, government contracts, and voting districts based on race will be impossible to enforce. . . .

Black Americans, these conservative writers claim, can be seen now as just another ethnic group, rather than as a distinctive racial group. As Stephan and Abigail Thernstrom write in *America in Black and White*,

> One of the sharpest distinctions between the experience of African Americans and of that of the more than 50 million immigrants who came voluntarily to the United States in the nineteenth and twentieth centuries is that blacks were not allowed into the marital melting pot that did so much to blur immigrant group consciousness and foster assimilation. Although [black activists] Louis Farrakhan and Spike Lee might not approve, that process has at last begun to affect African Americans in significant numbers.

Here rising intermarriage rates become proof that America has overcome its history of racist exclusions, even though the black-white marriage rate lags behind that of other types of interracial marriage. Some more realistic commentators insist that if interracial marriage rates are used as the indicator, blacks are not assimilating as successfully as Asians or Latinos, and they worry that a new American divide might emerge between blacks and nonblacks. Although such predictions are too pessimistic given the changes that have taken place since World War II, they serve as a reminder that old barriers can easily be replaced by newer, perhaps more insidious ones. . . .

Breaking Down Barriers

Perhaps the most important factor limiting the rate of black-white intermarriage is the kind of structural and institutionalized racism that the "love is the answer" discourse erases. Income inequality and school and residential segregation not only act as barriers preventing blacks and whites from meeting in situations that might lead to dating, but also continue the racial disadvantages that make blacks less attractive as marital partners. As long as there are real costs associated with being black, whites will think seriously before embarking on an interracial relationship. Marriage between blacks and whites will not become commonplace until race is no longer a marker of privilege or disadvantage.

The old segregationist fear that integration would lead to "race mixing" was well founded. Meaningful integration allows blacks and whites to meet, to transcend the cultural and historical legacies that hinder healthy relationships, and to marry if they so choose. There is no question that interracial love will become more common and even more accepted as racial barriers erode in American society, but it will take more than love to break down those barriers. Old hierarchies must be dismantled for new attitudes about interracial love and marriage to flourish.

"To foster a society and a civic life that respects difference . . . requires conscious commitment to the task."

Schools and Businesses Should Promote Diversity

Business–Higher Education Forum

The Business–Higher Education Forum (BHEF) is a membership organization of chief executives from American businesses, colleges and universities, and museums. The following viewpoint is excerpted from BHEF's 2002 report *Investing in People: Developing All of America's Talent on Campus and in the Workplace*. The forum argues that racial diversity benefits American educational institutions and businesses. The forum cites a range of studies showing that students who learn in racially diverse environments develop better critical thinking and interpersonal skills, and transfer these skills to the workplace. The BHEF also argues that businesses with diverse workforces are better able to adapt to an increasingly multicultural marketplace.

As you read, consider the following questions:

1. What are the three "democracy outcomes" demonstrated by students with diverse academic experience, according to researcher Patricia Gurin?
2. In the forum's view, why do educational institutions consider the "whole person" rather than just academic scores?
3. Why do culturally diverse workplaces tend to have better problem-solving capacities, according to author Taylor Cox?

Business–Higher Education Forum, *Investing in People: Developing All of America's Talent on Campus and in the Workplace*. Washington, DC: Business–Higher Education Forum, 2002. Copyright © 2002 by Business–Higher Education Forum. Reproduced by permission.

R acial and ethnic diversity has been a distinguishing char- acteristic of the United States since it became a nation.

More than 200 years after the Constitution was signed, more than 100 years after the Civil War, and some 30 years af- ter the peak of the civil rights movement, not only the results of Census 2000, but the debates over how to define racial and ethnic categories suggest that race still matters very much in America.

Yet even as the minority population increases, and official categories and definitions of racial and ethnic identity mul- tiply, there are many campuses and many places in the busi- ness world where members of minority groups are few and far between. Why should we care about this? Why should we want to be an inclusive society? The most basic, com- pelling answer is that America needs and promises equality of opportunity. An inclusive society is in keeping with our nation's values of fairness and justice, but it also is essential for our nation's economic competitiveness. . . .

Benefits to a Democratic Society

America is a society that places a high premium on personal and civic responsibility and participation by all citizens. As the nation's population becomes more diverse, it becomes increasingly important to ensure that all who reside in America, regardless of background, have the capacity and the opportunity to learn to live and work together.

Yet currently, many Americans live, grow up, and are ed- ucated in neighborhoods and schools where they have little or no meaningful interaction with people of other races. Es- pecially for students who grow up in racially, ethnically ho- mogeneous neighborhoods and schools, going to college may be the first time they are exposed, in a meaningful way, to people from other racial and ethnic backgrounds. For many, it may be the only opportunity for this kind of expo- sure before they enter the workplace and participate in civic life as adults. In *Making Choices for Multicultural Education: Five Approaches to Race, Class, and Gender*, Sleeter and Grant point out that students can learn most from those who have very different life experiences from theirs.

The evidence shows that encountering a range of racial,

ethnic, and cultural perspectives on campus enhances students' preparation for full participation in a democratic society, including the likelihood that they will live in communities that are not segregated after they leave college. Some of these specific benefits are discussed in a report prepared by University of Michigan psychology professor Patricia Y. Gurin. For the report, Gurin reviewed data from several research studies and identified the following three "democracy outcomes" that are demonstrated by both white and minority students who have a diverse academic experience.

Students who have had experience with diversity on campus demonstrate greater "citizenship engagement," meaning that they are more likely to participate in community and volunteer service, as well as in the political arena. As our society has become increasingly diverse, the need for leaders who represent the needs, interests, and perspectives of diverse communities has dramatically increased. Among the contributions that Gurin found to correlate with a diverse campus experience were influencing the political structure and influencing social values, as well as working in the community on issues such as helping others in difficulty, cleaning up the environment, and participating in community action programs.

Students who have had experience with diversity on campus demonstrate greater "racial/cultural engagement." This term refers to students' levels of cultural awareness, participation in activities that promote racial understanding, appreciation of other cultures, and acceptance of people from other cultures.

Students who have had experience with diversity on campus demonstrate greater "compatibility with differences." Understanding that different racial and ethnic groups share common values is a crucial preliminary step to being willing to manage differences so that they do not become divisive in our nation. The campus is one of the few places in our society where young people of different backgrounds can come to know one another and explore their commonalities as well as their differences. As Gurin concludes in her report, students "who participated in interactions with diverse peers were comfortable and prepared to live and work in a diverse society—an important goal of our educational mission."

As two other researchers have found, it is exposure to difference, in rich intellectual dialogues, and learning to live with difference that allows multicultural nations to succeed and prosper.

To foster a society and a civic life that respects difference, that welcomes and benefits from the talents, perspectives, and life experiences of all of our citizens, requires conscious commitment to the task. One of the most effective ways to carry out that commitment is to ensure that the doors of higher education are open to all who are qualified to pass through them. Another is to ensure that once students are on campus, they have access to a diverse faculty and out-of-classroom resources and interactions that will equip them to be successful and productive in their careers and to contribute to America's civic and social life.

Benefits to Learning

Racial and ethnic diversity on campus enhances the learning environment for everyone.

The University of Notre Dame's "Statement on Diversity" says it well: "Notre Dame's goal of increasing diversity is wholly consistent with its commitment to academic excellence. In fact, attaining a diverse faculty and staff is essential to the educational mission. . . ."

In recent years, higher education has embraced racial and ethnic diversity as an essential component of quality and success in academe. As Bowen and Bok wrote in *The Shape of the River*, "What admissions officers must decide is which set of applicants, considered individually and collectively, will take fullest advantage of what the college has to offer, contribute most to the educational process in college, and be most successful in using what they have learned for the benefit of the larger society."

Institutions that consider the whole person—including the facets of an applicant's background that can materially contribute to a robust exchange of ideas and improved learning by all students—do so because they believe that a diverse student body and faculty are crucial to fulfilling the mission of higher education.

In a February 2001 speech to the American Council on

Education, Richard C. Atkinson, president of the University of California, reflected the opinion of many in higher education when he said that instead of "narrowly defined quantitative formulas," based largely on test scores, campuses should "adopt procedures that look at applicants in a comprehensive, holistic way."

The Public Supports Diversity in Higher Education

How important do you personally believe it is to have students of different races, cultures, and backgrounds in higher education/elementary and secondary school education—very important, somewhat important, not very important, or not at all important?

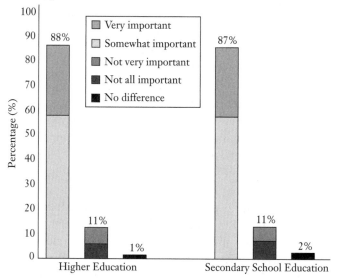

American Council on Education/Business–Higher Education Forum, nationwide survey on 975 registered voters, Lake Snell Perry & Associates, August 13, 2000.

The validity of basing admissions decisions on criteria that value the whole person—not just the part of the person that performs well on standardized tests—is bolstered by numerous studies showing that learning benefits accrue to both white and minority students who come in contact with people of diverse backgrounds and with diverse ideas and information.

Students who are exposed to people with a range of backgrounds and ideas are better critical thinkers than those who have less contact with diversity. In her report, Gurin found that students who "experienced the most racial and ethnic diversity in classroom settings and in informal interactions with peers showed the greatest engagement in active thinking processes, growth in intellectual engagement and motivation, and growth in intellectual and academic skills." A series of studies by E.T. Pascarella and others analyzed the impact of students' experiences with campus diversity at various points in their college career. They found that students who had interacted with students from other racial and ethnic backgrounds, or who had attended workshops on racial and cultural awareness, were better critical thinkers and more open to challenge in their discussions than those who did not have these experiences.

Students who are exposed to people with a range of backgrounds and ideas are more likely to show greater social and interpersonal development than students with less exposure to diversity. Most students come to college at a time when the personality and identity that will define them for years to come are still being formed. Because students are at this critical developmental stage, Gurin's study demonstrates, exposure to diverse groups, experiences, and ideas can have a long-term, even lifelong, effect on their openness to multiple viewpoints and to active participation in a diverse society.

Students and faculty perceive the benefits of campus diversity for learning. In *Making the Most of College*, his recent book based on interviews with students about their campus experiences, Richard J. Light writes: "Every undergraduate I interviewed believes he or she has something unique and valuable to contribute. . . . This conviction of having something to offer, along with an enthusiasm about interacting with students whose backgrounds differ from their own, is widespread among undergraduates from all ethnic and racial groups."

Such findings are not limited to undergraduates. For example, a survey of law students at Harvard and the University of Michigan found that 90 percent of the students felt that their exposure to racial and ethnic diversity at school—especially being able to engage in discussions with students of different perspectives—had enhanced their learning. Similarly, a national survey of 55,000 college and university faculty members by the Higher Education Research Institute at UCLA reported that 90 percent of the respondents agreed with the statement that "a racially/ethnically diverse student body enhances the educational experiences of all students.". . .

Benefits to Business and the Economy

To a large extent, business and the nation's economy as a whole depend on graduates of higher education for success. The benefits that accrue to college graduates who are exposed to racial and ethnic diversity during their education carry over directly into the work environment. The improved ability to think critically, to understand issues from different points of view, and to collaborate harmoniously with co-workers from a wide range of cultural backgrounds all enhance a college graduate's ability to contribute to his or her company's growth and productivity.

These skills are essential to the nation's success in both the domestic and global economies. With our increasingly diverse population, success in the domestic economy depends more than ever on the ability of businesses to adapt their services and products, as well as their marketing strategies, to appeal to customers from a wide range of cultural backgrounds. At the same time, as international economic barriers continue to fall, the imperative to ensure that all American students are prepared to participate in the global economy has accelerated. According to the Hudson Institute, "By the mid-1990s . . . foreign trade played a role in the American economy that was between two and three times as important as it had been in 1965."

When the Rand Corporation interviewed representatives of 16 corporations about the qualities they seek in the people they recruit, several of the qualities they mentioned were the same as the benefits that have been shown to result from being educated in a racially and ethnically diverse environment: problem-solving skills, the ability to work well with diverse colleagues, and openness to new ideas.

The corporate resources, human and financial, that have been invested in recruiting and preparing more members of minorities for the workforce, and the proliferation of workplace diversity programs, attest that many American business leaders believe that in their world, racial and ethnic diversity brings value to their enterprises—and that they look to higher education to prepare the workers who have the academic, social, and interpersonal skills they need to succeed in this world. . . .

What exactly does racial and ethnic diversity contribute to American business? The following are some of the answers that have emerged from interviews with corporate leaders, research studies that have examined these issues, and corporate mission statements and public relations materials.

Education of members of racial and ethnic minorities benefits the economy as a whole. Educational attainment is directly related to job opportunities and salary levels. [Educational Testing Service] estimates that raising the educational attainment of members of underrepresented minorities could strike a huge blow against poverty and for higher income for millions of Americans. According to ETS, "If Hispanics and African Americans had the same education and commensurate earnings as whites, the earnings of Hispanic men would increase by 71 percent, Hispanic women by 34 percent, African-American men by 53 percent, and African-American women by 15 percent," spurring "an upsurge of national wealth" that would amount to $113 billion annually for African Americans and $118 billion for Hispanics, and enormously contributing to the vitality of the national economy.

Education in a diverse environment enhances the creativity, innovation, and problem-solving skills that graduates bring to their jobs. Employees who can view problems from a variety of perspectives, participate in and stimulate creative thinking, and effectively collaborate with a diverse group of colleagues, are invaluable to businesses. Employees who are exposed to people with a range of backgrounds and ideas are more likely to understand issues from different points of view. This ability is an important factor in the capacity of organizations to perform their work successfully. In his book, *Cultural Diversity in Organizations*, Taylor Cox reviewed a series of studies comparing the effectiveness of homogeneous groups with those of more diverse groups in seeking solutions to a variety of problems. The evidence from the studies suggested that the participation of people with different perspectives and backgrounds improved the quality of both the problem-solving process and the solutions generated. Cox concluded that "culturally diverse workforces have the potential to solve problems better because of several factors: a greater variety of perspectives brought to bear on the issue, a higher level of analysis of alternatives, and a lower probability of group-think."

Employees of different racial and ethnic backgrounds can offer important perspectives to the development of products and services designed for an increasingly diverse marketplace. Population projections show that the domestic market in the United States is becoming increasingly multicultural. The Selig Center for Economic Growth at the University of Georgia reports that by 2001, the total buying power of African Americans, American Indians, and Asians will reach $861 billion, a 96 percent increase over the estimated $440 billion in 1990. Over the same period of time, the buying power of Hispanics will have grown from its 1990 level of $207.5 billion to a projected 2001 level of $452.4 billion.

American businesses now participate in global markets to an unprecedented degree. One of the corporate representatives interviewed for the Rand Corporation report summed up the significance of "globalism" as "a complete revolution in the thought process. . . . The economic world doesn't revolve around the United States—the United States is one among many strong players in the global business environment." In this environment, employees who have studied and lived with people from a range of racial, ethnic, and cultural backgrounds are better prepared to collaborate with colleagues around the globe, as well as to perceive and respond to worldwide business opportunities. According to Rob Norton, senior vice president of human resources for Pfizer Inc., "When we bring different ideas, different constructs, and different cultural backgrounds to the table, the outcome is powerful.". . .

As our nation becomes increasingly more diverse, the record becomes clearer: The positive effects of diversity are broad and touch our lives in many ways. All that stands between us and even greater benefits for our society in the future is the willingness to acknowledge our differences and the commitment to respond to the challenges and opportunities they present.

*"The drive of elite institutions to fill their
token roster of minorities, no matter the
costs to the tokens or to their own
standards, . . . [gives] a false impression."*

Schools and Businesses Should Not Promote Diversity

Heather Mac Donald

Heather Mac Donald is a contributing editor for *City Journal*
and the author of the book *Are Cops Racist?* In the following
viewpoint she argues that businesses' and universities' obses-
sion with creating racially diverse campuses and workplaces
harms both minorities and society as a whole. Many businesses
and universities, she contends, cannot find enough qualified
minority applicants, so they lower their standards. The poorly
qualified minority students then often drop out of the school,
she notes, or perform at a lower level than their coworkers.
Organizations have embraced diversity-centered policies, she
concludes, as a way of avoiding discussion of the real problem:
the dearth of qualified black and Hispanic applicants.

As you read, consider the following questions:

1. What proportion of minority law students admitted
   under affirmative action policies in 1991 dropped out,
   according to Mac Donald?
2. Why do over 60 percent of minorities report
   experiencing "race-related barriers" to professional
   advancement, in the author's opinion?

A recent pseudo-scandal at the Justice Department is yet another depressing reminder of intractable racial taboos —although not the kind we usually hear about from hand-wringing pundits and civil-rights scolds.

At the end of October [2003], the *New York Times* accused the Justice Department of covering up a study critical of its "diversity" hiring and management. The department had posted the study—a $360,000 piece of boilerplate from the diversity-consulting industry—on its website. About half the text had been very visibly blacked out. Among the redacted portions, gleefully reported on the *Times*'s front page, were such standard "diversity" findings as the fact that more minority lawyers than white ones perceive "stereotyping, harassment and racial tension" in their workplace.

For the *Times* and likeminded [George W.] Bush administration critics, the story was a glorious twofer: Not only was Attorney General John Ashcroft, that scourge of civil rights, abusing his minority employees, but he was trying to conceal it. Senator Edward Kennedy blasted the department for ignoring "diversity" issues. Representatives John Conyers Jr. and Jerrold Nadler issued a demand, in self-professed "outrage," that the Justice Department's inspector general investigate Diversitygate.

This scandal was a fake. The missing portions of the diversity study (later exhumed by a computer sleuth) had been redacted for a perfectly good reason: A rule in the Freedom of Information Act exempts advisory and "predecisional" material from disclosure. The deletions contained positive information about the department, just as the posted text contained "negative" findings, such as the higher attrition rate of minority hires.

The Diversity Charade

But there was a scandal in the episode, albeit a longstanding one: the enduring charade about minority underachievement in the workplace. Every month, businesses and government agencies lavish vast sums on diversity "consultants" to come up with every reason other than the correct one— the skills gap—for why they do not have a proportional number of black and Hispanic employees. And, just as regularly, elite opinion-makers hold up the results of such sham studies as proof of American racism.

The Justice Department's recent diversity study, produced by KPMG Consulting, was a classic of the genre. Here was page after page of complicated graphs calculating to the hundredth of a percentage point the ratio of black, Hispanic, and female attorneys in every possible position within the department. Here was the disparagement of the white male "dominant culture norms," along with the call to "be more creative about defining qualifications" (i.e., to gut standards for minorities). Here was the inevitable push for tying the pay of managers to their promotion of minorities. But, above all else, here was the scrupulous, all-encompassing silence on every page of the document about why this futile exercise was undertaken in the first place: the dearth of qualified minority attorneys to fill those minutely tabulated Justice Department slots.

The real missing data from the Justice diversity study are these: In 2002, only 29 black applicants were qualified without a racial boost for a top-ten law school (from which the elite branches of the Justice Department recruit), compared with 4,500 college seniors nationwide, as Jonathan Kay has reported in *Commentary*. The situation was identical a decade ago: Only 24 black applicants met the academic requirements for the top 10 percent of law schools in 1991, according to Stephan and Abigail Thernstrom. Naturally, those schools were not about to let the lack of preparedness among minority applicants stand in the way of demonstrating the schools' high-minded embrace of racial balance. They admitted 420 blacks to their first-year classes anyway, thus ensuring that nearly all would start out with a disadvantage compared with their white and Asian peers.

The results of such racial double standards are predictable: Over a fifth of affirmative-action law students from the 1991 cohort, for example, dropped out. With few exceptions, black students post grades near the bottom of their class. As a result, almost none qualify for law review. The bar exam failure rate for affirmative-action beneficiaries is far higher than for merit-based admits. Nearly a third of the 1991 quota admits failed after three attempts, a rate seven times that of whites, according to the Thernstroms.

Ignoring the Racial Skills Gap

The racial charade requires that law-school administrators express deep puzzlement about such facts, even though their own admissions policies produced the disparity. The dean of Vanderbilt Law School, Kent D. Syverud, recently told the *Chronicle of Higher Education* that the lack of minority representation on the school's law journals is "one of the biggest challenges I've faced as dean." Yet Syverud defended the use of racial preferences in law-school admissions in the [June 2003] Supreme Court affirmative action case *Grutter v. Bollinger*,[1] so he is merely reaping what he has sown. True to form, many law schools, like New York University and the University of Pennsylvania, have rejiggered traditional law-review requirements to guarantee the presence of face-saving blacks and Hispanics on the review masthead.

The genius of the diversity charade is to turn a supply problem into a demand problem. The reason the Justice Department does not have a proportional sampling of black and Hispanic attorneys is simple: The numbers just aren't there. But the diversity industry tells us that the real reason behind the lack of racial proportionality is demand: Employers are not trying hard enough to recruit minority employees, and when they do hire them, they subject them to racism—which can be rooted out only by more diversity-industry interventions.

A fail-safe source for proving work-site racism is the minority employee survey. In 1990, New York's most exclusive law firms noticed that they didn't have many black partners. The obvious explanation—inadequate supply of partnership material—was taboo from the start. So New York's legal titans began the arduous process of ignoring the obvious. Working through the bar association, they hived off into a decade-long series of diversity committees and subcommittees, among whose initiatives was a poll of minority associates about their work experiences. Eureka! Here was an explanation for low minority headcount that the firms could live with: According to the subcommittee on minority retention, over 60 percent of black lawyers reported "race-

---

1. The Supreme Court upheld the University of Michigan Law School's admissions program.

related barriers to their professional development." Similarly, the recent Justice Department diversity study found that "significantly more" minorities perceived racism on the job than whites.

The Red Herring of Racism

Now what is the cause of this perception? It may of course be the case that these elite employers, despite their years of schooling in the country's most liberal institutions and despite their strenuous efforts to find as many black employees as they can, are in fact racist. But here is an alternative possibility: Affirmative-action beneficiaries, having been admitted to organizations for which they are significantly less qualified than their peers, experience difficulties performing up to the norm and attribute those difficulties to their environment. Find an honest partner at a high-powered law firm, for example, and he will acknowledge, only on deep background, that many black associates struggle mightily with legal writing. But racial prejudice is the easy culprit—and little wonder. Minority students are fed a steady diet of victimology in colleges and law schools. Critical Race Studies courses in law schools, for example, maintain that legal rationality silences the minority voice. So, it is hardly surprising that overmatched minority attorneys blame bias for their plight.

The diversity charade's most bizarre feature is this: Employers and universities would rather take the rap for racism than tell the truth about minority underperformance. After the poll showing that black New York attorneys blame their firms' bigotry for their lack of advancement, the most that those firms would meekly say in their own defense was that such "perceptions are not based on the animus that we normally associate with racial discrimination." An understatement, if there ever was one.

Far from possessing "animus" against blacks, New York's most prestigious firms, like the law elite everywhere, spend hundreds of thousands of dollars a year on diversity recruiting, diversity support groups, and diversity social functions like the party hosted last fall by the firm Paul Weiss. Young minority law associates from across the city were invited. The fancy Judson Grill was rented out, John Payton, the black attorney who argued *Grutter* spoke (gloating about the victory), and guests left with goody bags containing diversity paperweights, copies of the *Grutter* opinion, and a magazine called *Diversity Inc.* with articles on how to tell if firms value—you guessed it—diversity.

Two Problems with Racial Favoritism

Racial preferences in college, though they seem a shortcut to a multi-ethnic elite, actually fail that test on two grounds. First, they systematically mismatch minority talent to academic opportunities, placing the top 10 percent of designated minority students into competition with the top 1 percent of white and Asian students. Not surprisingly, a disproportionately high number of minority students then drop out—and those who remain are tempted to explain their difficulties as a result of concealed racism. Hence the classrooms of diversity are often places of resentment and division rather than of the energetic exchange of life experiences. . . . In order to ensure that these failures do not prevent the emergence of a multi-ethnic elite, therefore, the system of race preferences has to be continued in some form or other after college.

Which leads logically to the second problem. If the new multi-ethnic elite is to be accepted in its leadership role, then Americans must feel that it is a genuine elite rooted in merit. . . . If the suspicion grows that this is an engineered elite, then the elite will be under permanent suspicion, resulting in widespread cynicism. Yet a system of permanent racial preferences is exactly that: the engineering of an elite. A secondary result of this, as Justice Clarence Thomas and others have noted, is that non-engineered members of the elite come under suspicion too as the probable beneficiaries of racial favoritism.

John O'Sullivan, *National Review*, July 28, 2003.

But faced with the choice of copping to bias or explaining the difficulty of finding qualified minority applicants, there's not a prominent organization that won't fall on its sword as a racist. . . . And so the New York Bar, skewered by its black associates, dutifully ordered itself into diversity training and set itself ever more rigorous hiring and promotion goals, as if its members hadn't already been frantically trying to find and promote black attorneys. Likewise, the Justice Department, accused by its minority employees of "harassment and stereotyping" and accused by the press of not hiring and promoting enough minorities, has merely hung its head and promised to do better through new undertakings like a loan repayment program and more "equitable" assignment of cases.

Although an event sometimes forces momentary honesty about the skills gap, the racial taboo always triumphs in the end. While covering the recent Supreme Court affirmative-action challenges, for example, even the liberal media could hardly avoid mentioning the 200-point SAT gap between whites and Asians, on the one hand, and blacks and Hispanics on the other. But those moments pass without a trace, and the *New York Times* and other press outlets quickly go back to reporting on the underrepresentation of minorities in this or that organization as a sign of bias, as the *Wall Street Journal* did in November [2003], informing readers that "high turnover among people of color" suggests the employer does not value diversity.

Covering Up the Real Problem

The drive of elite institutions to fill their token roster of minorities, no matter the costs to the tokens or to their own standards, only perpetuates the racial taboo by giving a false impression. The smattering of black and Hispanic faces on the bench, in law and medical school classes, and on the brochures of selective colleges makes it harder for the public to grasp how severely minorities lag behind the norm in reading and math. Worse, preferences keep the institutions that use them on the sidelines of educational reform and cultural change. Remove their ability to practice racial window-dressing, however, and many would try to actually shrink the skills gap rather than just cover it up.

The only time the University of California system sought to systematically improve California's abysmal schools was after the U.C. Regents, in 1995, banned the use of race in admissions. In response, university administrators launched a massive outreach program into high schools and elementary schools to prepare minority students for competitive enrollment. Had the Supreme Court struck down educational preferences this summer, many colleges, law schools, law firms, and businesses would have been forced into a similar crusade

—at least until the next dodge for covertly reinstating quotas had emerged.

In her recent decision upholding affirmative action, Supreme Court Justice Sandra Day O'Connor gave colleges and law schools 25 years to continue papering over the racial skills gap. Expect another 25 years of inaction on minority skills, more pseudo-scandals about low minority representation, and an ever fatter diversity industry laughing all the way to the bank.

"The decision of the U.S. Supreme Court in Grutter v. Bollinger *is disheartening in the extreme."*

Race-Based College Admissions Policies Should Be Banned

Carl Cohen

Carl Cohen is a professor of philosophy at the University of Michigan and coauthor of *Affirmative Action and Racial Preference: A Debate*. In the following viewpoint he discusses two June 2003 Supreme Court decisions that he believes are contradictory and harmful. In *Gratz v. Bollinger*, the Court ruled that the University of Michigan's point-based undergraduate admissions system was unconstitutional because it awarded points based on race, thus violating the Fourteenth Amendment and civil rights laws. But in *Grutter v. Bollinger* the Court ruled that the University of Michigan Law School's system, which treats minority status as a "plus factor" in a more individualized applicant review process, was constitutional. Cohen concludes that since the Court failed to completely ban race-based admissions policies, legislators should take it upon themselves to prohibit such policies.

As you read, consider the following questions:

1. What two-pronged standard must a race-based admissions policy adhere to, according to the author?
2. In *Grutter v. Bollinger*, what did the Court decide was a "compelling state interest," as quoted by Cohen?
3. How many years more did the Court feel that race-based admissions policies will be necessary, according to Cohen?

Carl Cohen, "Winks, Nods, Disguises—and Racial Preference," *Commentary*, vol. 116, September 2003, p. 34. Copyright © 2003 by the American Jewish Committee. All rights reserved. Reproduced by permission of the publisher and the author.

[I n 1978] when the case of *Bakke v. University of California* arrived before the U.S. Supreme Court, it was widely anticipated that the Justices would at last resolve an issue that had been bedeviling the country for years: the permissibility of preference by race in university admissions. It did not happen. To the contrary, the internal divisions of the Court at that time, as reflected in six tangled opinions, left the matter in a more muddled condition than it already was. True, Allan Bakke, the white applicant who had been turned down by the University of California in favor of less qualified minority candidates, won his suit; naked racial preference was thrown out. But what other sorts of racial and ethnic preferences might be permitted was left quite uncertain.

The chief muddler in 1978 was Justice Lewis Powell, a decent man and an honorable judge who found racial discrimination appalling and unconstitutional and yet also felt that he had to permit some wiggle room for college admissions officers, to attend to race under some circumstances. In his long and convoluted opinion, notorious for the confusion to which it subsequently gave rise, Powell held that it would be reasonable for a university to take into consideration the race of particular applicants for the sake of achieving intellectual "diversity" in the student body. To treat people in general differently because of their color, Powell said, was plainly a violation of the equal-protection clause of the Fourteenth Amendment. But to allow the race of individual applicants to weigh in their favor for the sake of diversity did not amount to such a violation.

No other Justice joined Powell in his confused and rather fanciful homage to the concept of diversity. And yet his principle took root. This was in part because, in a Court divided between two parties of four, his had been the deciding voice. For the universities, the problem with *Bakke* was that it unambiguously rejected preferences for the sake of remedying past injustices committed against racial minorities—precisely the defense that, until then, many universities had been relying upon. If they were determined to go on giving preference, as for the most part they were, they would henceforth have to lean upon the weak reed of Powell's speculations concerning diversity. And this, for the next quarter-century, they proceeded to do.

Problems with the Diversity Defense

But would the "diversity defense" withstand renewed constitutional challenge? That central question was presented to the Supreme Court in two cases involving the University of Michigan and finally decided this past June [2003]: *Gratz v. Bollinger*, concerning the admissions practices of Michigan's undergraduate college, and *Grutter v. Bollinger*, concerning the admissions practices of its law school. ("Bollinger" is Lee Bollinger, formerly the president of the university.) Though the two cases differed significantly in their particulars, in each case the university justified its practice of using racial preferences on the grounds not of remediation but of diversity.

One would have thought—I certainly thought—that the university would have an extremely tough time of it. For any state to treat people differently by race is an odious practice, presumptively unconstitutional and hence subject to the rigorous standard of "strict scrutiny" applied to any putative exceptions to the rule. That standard has two prongs. To win file day, the university would need five of the nine Justices to agree both that racial diversity was a "compelling" need of the state of Michigan and that the system of preference it was using had been "narrowly tailored" to meet that compelling need.

How could it do that? It seemed eminently plain that the state's need for racial diversity in its university, if it had any such need at all, was not compelling under any ordinary meaning of that term. Moreover, the two Michigan systems giving preference, so far from being narrowly tailored, were (as one federal judge had earlier put it) more like a chain saw than a sewing machine in their mode of operation. Success for the University of Michigan thus seemed very unlikely indeed. . . .

In *Gratz v. Bollinger*, the Supreme Court of the United States did hold that the numerical admissions system used by Michigan's undergraduate college, in which a given number of points was awarded to all applicants in certain ethnic categories, violated the equal-protection clause of the Fourteenth Amendment as well as the Civil Rights Act of 1964. But on the same day, in *Grutter v. Bollinger*, the Court held that "the educational benefits that flow from a diverse student body" were indeed, in the context of higher education, a compelling state interest. Moreover, the particular form of deliberate racial discrimination practiced by the law school of the University of Michigan was found to be consistent with the constitutional guarantee of equal protection of the laws.

Asay. © 2003 by Creators Syndicate, Inc. Reproduced by permission.

The diversity principle, even if only in one context, and with heavy restrictions, has thus been embedded in law; Powell's weak reed has become a mighty limb. In the meantime, in the tension between these two latest decisions, what was muddy in *Bakke* has become muddier still. . . .

Narrowly Tailored

According to the University of Michigan, the educational benefits of diversity were said to flow from the creation of a "critical mass" of minority representatives in the student body: a number sufficiently large that the members of a given minority in a given class would not feel themselves "isolated" in that class. The racial instrument used in law-school admissions was, the university held, narrowly tailored to this end. Unlike the practice in the undergraduate college, the law school, in evaluating applicants, claimed not to rely on some fixed numerical value mechanically awarded to every member of certain ethnic groups. Instead the critical masses needed for the three designated minorities—African-Americans, Native Americans and Hispanics—were said to have been artfully assembled through the use of highly sensitive reviews of each individual applicant. . . .

The *Grutter* majority accepted the sham whole hog. Baldly asserting that student-body ethnic diversity was a compelling state need, it found this end narrowly served by a process in which, allegedly, ethnicity was considered as no more than a "plus factor" in the files of "particular applicants," all the attributes of each applicant being "holistically" appraised and "all pertinent elements of diversity considered in light of the particular qualifications of each applicant" in the quest for a critical mass. (The language is that of Justice Sandra Day O'Connor in her majority opinion.) On this reading, the fact that, of two law-school applicants with identical academic credentials, a black applicant's chances of admission were in fact hundreds of times greater than those of a white applicant must be regarded as no more than a coincidence.

If this is strict scrutiny, the term is without meaning.

Thanks to the Court's decision, still worse is now to come. The law-school system, a sham in reality, has been elevated to the status of a model—and not only for law schools. As we have seen, Michigan's use of race in undergraduate admissions, which did not pretend to be "individualized" or "holistic," was on that account found to be flatly unconstitutional. But henceforth, Michigan and many other universities will formulate their undergraduate preferential schemes in phrases echoing the language of the law-school program. Beginning now, "individualized review," "holistic," "critical mass," "plus factor," "a particular applicant's file," and the like will appear ubiquitously and talismanically in the description of admission systems from coast to coast.

The Quota System Lives On

Of course, it will be far easier to profess such highly individualized review systems than to realize them. And so a second-level sham will be explicitly invited: a fraud imitating a fraud.

Consider: the law school at Michigan enrolls some 350

182

new students each year. Of the several thousand who apply, a good number are speedily disqualified, with many of the remaining applicants interviewed in person and the complete file of every admitted applicant examined by a single person, the assistant dean for admissions. Even though, at the Michigan law school, the real goal has been racial balancing, the requisite process of "individualization," as approved by the Court, is conceivably doable, if with some strain.

The undergraduate college at Michigan is a rather different affair. It receives more than 25,000 applications for admission each year. Picture a gymnasium in which those fat application files are stacked in piles six feet high; there will be some 350 of these piles, or more, pretty nearly stuffing the gymnasium to the gills. Now imagine that each application is to be evaluated comparatively, with race and many other factors given varying and appropriate weights in the assessment of each candidate. Remember, no numerical value for ethnicity is to be assigned, no quantitative system applied.

How, in the name of reason, is the comparison of these 25,000 applicants to be carried out? Even for an army of admissions officers, the exercise would be hopeless. It is utterly impossible for the University of Michigan—not to speak of universities in Minnesota and Ohio and other states where undergraduate colleges are substantially larger still—to review all the particular qualifications of each of tens of thousands of applicants, weighing race as but one factor, without using some numerical calculus. Any future claim to that effect is guaranteed to be a deception.

In its written argument defending the mechanical award of points for race in undergraduate admissions, the University of Michigan granted candidly that "the volume of applications and the presentation of applicant information make it impractical for [the undergraduate college] to use the . . . admissions system" of the law school. Of course. That is why the university argued, in effect, that since the racial results it sought could only be achieved using a system of numerical weights, such a system must be permissible, for there is no other way to achieve the approved aim of diversity.

No! responded the Court in *Gratz*. The use of race is permitted in some ways, but it is not urged, and you are certainly not entitled to do whatever you think is required. The Court's strictures were not to be bypassed: a university may not "employ whatever means it desires to achieve the stated goal of diversity without regard to the limits imposed by our strict-scrutiny analysis." Nor did "the fact that the implementation of a program providing individualized consideration might present administrative challenges . . . render constitutional an otherwise problematic system." So, under *Gratz*, the university has been forbidden to do what it asserts it must do in order to achieve the racial objective it asserts it must pursue and which, under *Grutter*, has now been found "compelling." Here, in the pull of the two decisions against each other, is indeed a recipe for still more pervasive obfuscation and more shameful hypocrisy. . . .

Government-Sanctioned Racial Discrimination Must End

To be sure, there are some signs of judicial distress. Even Justice O'Connor, who in *Grutter* found race preference tolerable, reluctantly acknowledged that "there are serious problems of justice connected with the idea of preference itself." These are precisely the problems that will saddle universities, and American society, for years to come.

How many years? The Court accepted the assurances of the University of Michigan that the racial discrimination it now practices must some day end. The firmly expressed expectation of the Court is that this will happen within 25 years (a piety to which Justice Thomas retorted that the principle of equality ought not have to wait a quarter of a century to be vindicated). In the meantime what lies ahead is the agony of a long chain of public disputes. For one thing, there will be no end of quarreling over the systems of preference being given. Although the universities will claim the protection of the words used in *Grutter* it will be very hard to hide the reality of their practices, and these will be subjected to continuing adverse scrutiny. We may thus be reasonably certain that Michigan and those of its sister institutions likewise relying upon allegedly nonquantified diversity as the justification for preferences will be back in court again and again.

But the controversy will also move from the courtroom to

the ballot box. If the Supreme Court has found that, in the interest of diversity, race preference may be given, it remains for the people of the several states to decide for themselves whether, in their state, race preference is to be forbidden. In Michigan, for example, every effort will be made by the time of the presidential election of 2004 to place on the ballot a Michigan Civil Rights Initiative—an equivalent of California's Proposition 209. [Editor's note: The initiative was not on Michigan's 2004 ballot; supporters are now aiming for 2006.] The operative sentence in that proposition, now incorporated in the California constitution, is nearly identical to a critical passage of the Civil Rights Act of 1964, with the addition of five words that appear here in emphasis. It reads:

> The state shall not discriminate against, *or grant preferential treatment to*, any individual or group on the basis of race, sex, color, ethnicity, or national origin in the operation of public employment, public education, or public contracting.

Once the matter is on the ballot, it will also become more difficult for legislators and political candidates to dodge this controversy as they have so often done in the past. Will they urge their constituents to vote against a proposition forbidding race preference? If so, must we not conclude that they support race preference?

The decision of the U.S. Supreme Court in *Grutter v. Bollinger* is disheartening in the extreme. But the governing rule in this matter will come ultimately from the citizenry, and we must trust that the large majority of Americans, as reported in survey after survey and confirmed in election after election, continues to find racism of every sort disgusting. I was wrong about the outcome of the battle in court; now the war must move to other fronts.

"The demand that universities look like America is too powerful to be uprooted by a judicial command."

Race-Based College Admissions Policies Should Not Be Banned

Jeffrey Rosen

Jeffrey Rosen is a writer for the *New Republic*, a weekly political magazine. In the following viewpoint he defends the Supreme Court's June 2003 decision (in *Grutter v. Bollinger*) to uphold race-based college admissions policies as constitutional. The Court's 2003 decision, he explains, stems from the 1978 *Bakke* decision, which holds that colleges and universities may, in some circumstances, consider race as a factor in their admissions policies. Conservative members of the Court wanted to overturn that decision, but Rosen argues that that their view is an extreme, questionable one that most Americans do not share.

As you read, consider the following questions:

1. In summing up Justice Sandra Day O'Connor's majority opinion, how does Rosen describe the conclusion she reached?
2. In Rosen's view, what two goals do Justice Clarence Thomas and other conservatives believe universities should be forced to choose between?
3. In the face of widespread disagreement about racial preferences, to what institutions does the author believe that judges should defer?

Jeffrey Rosen, "Getting Affirmative Action Right: Light Footprint," *The New Republic*, July 7, 2003. Copyright © 2003 by The New Republic, Inc. Reproduced by permission.

In the months leading up to the [June 2003] Supreme Court decision on affirmative action, it was hard not to feel a sense of dread. At other great moments of constitutional drama—the decision to reaffirm *Roe* in 1992 and to settle the presidential election of 2000—the justices had allowed an inflated sense of their own importance to distort their judgment and compromise their reasoning. On both occasions, their moment in the national spotlight diminished them: The Court short-circuited important political debates without firmly rooting their intervention in constitutional principles that people on both sides of the debate could readily understand.

On affirmative action, there was a similar danger that the Court might intervene heavy-handedly in an area where the country was hardly clamoring for judicial intervention. Universities had more or less made their peace with the flawed *Bakke* decision [allowing affirmative action to promote diversity], and even the Bush administration had clearly signaled that the last thing it wanted was a principled decision striking down affirmative action in all its forms. There was every reason to fear that the swing justice, Sandra Day O'Connor, would reprise her role in the abortion case by crafting a novel and muddled compromise that both gave her the last word on a bitter national debate and made the polarization far worse.

Treading Lightly Around a Complex Issue

But O'Connor resisted temptation. Instead of trying to put her own stamp on affirmative action—as she did on abortion when she invented a new standard for measuring restrictions—O'Connor candidly acknowledged the complexity of the political and legal challenges universities face as they struggle to balance the competing values of color-blindness, diversity, and academic excellence. In the 25 years since the Court last confronted affirmative action in higher education, political pressures to ensure that universities look like America have proved to be so intense that, when courts and legislators have banned affirmative action, the best public universities have refused to accept the resulting decline in the number of minority students that inevitably follows. Instead, they have lowered academic standards across the board, thereby preserving minority enrollment at the cost of destroying their selective admissions standards.

Rather than forcing universities to choose between selectivity and diversity, O'Connor said they had a constitutionally compelling interest in achieving both. Writing for a majority of her colleagues—she was joined by Justices John Paul Stevens, David Souter, Stephen Breyer, and Ruth Bader Ginsburg—she upheld the University of Michigan Law School's affirmative action program (which seeks a "critical mass" of minority students to achieve the intellectual benefits of educational diversity) and reaffirmed Justice Lewis Powell's *Bakke* opinion in unequivocal terms. But, unlike her coy performance in reaffirming *Roe*, where she upheld the result without endorsing its reasoning, O'Connor made clear she agreed with the core holding of *Bakke*—that universities have a compelling interest in the educational benefits that flow from racial diversity. To preserve the educational autonomy that the First Amendment protects, O'Connor concluded, judges should defer to the judgments of educators about how best to fulfill their educational mission.

At the same time that she reaffirmed *Bakke*, O'Connor's opinion for the Court made clear that she and her colleagues take the strictures of *Bakke* seriously. Justice Powell had stressed that race couldn't be used to insulate minority candidates from competitive consideration with other applicants. Emphasizing the importance of treating each applicant as an individual, O'Connor and Breyer joined their four conservative colleagues—Justices William Rehnquist, Anthony Kennedy, Clarence Thomas, and Antonin Scalia—in rejecting the University of Michigan's undergraduate admissions policy. The 20-point automatic boost that all minority applicants receive, these justices held, precludes the university from assessing the particular contribution to educational diversity that each individual applicant brings to the table.

Some Fuzziness Is Acceptable

It's true that the Court has perpetuated the inherent fuzziness of *Bakke* rather than frankly acknowledging its analytical weaknesses. While Justice Powell insisted that race could be a "plus factor" but not a rigid quota in admissions, the difference between the two is often hard to discern. As Chief Justice Rehnquist noted in his dissent from the law school case, the number of admitted African American and Hispanic students—which the university calls a "critical mass"—has been consistently (and suspiciously) proportionate to the number of African Americans and Hispanics in the applicant pool. Moreover, given the magnitude of the score gaps between African Americans and Hispanic students and their white and Asian counterparts, it's hard to avoid the conclusion that race is as decisive a factor for admitting many of the minority law school applicants as it is for admitting the undergraduate applicants. The most obvious difference is that the undergraduate admissions program assigns a numerical value to its racial preferences while the law school doesn't.

In her dissent to the undergraduate case, Justice Ginsburg suggested the Court should have allowed universities to be candid about the degree of their racial preferences, rather than forcing them to lie. "If honesty is the best policy, surely Michigan's accurately described, fully disclosed College affirmative action program is preferable to achieving similar numbers through winks, nods, and disguises," Ginsburg argued. She noted persuasively that schools such as Rice University in Texas that have been prohibited from taking race into account explicitly have resorted to camouflages, such as asking applicants to write self-pitying essays about their "cultural traditions" or their successes in overcoming victimhood. But, if the Court removed all constitutional requirements that applicants be evaluated as individuals, universities would almost certainly resort to crudely statistical, two-track admissions systems that fail to compare white and black applicants in a meaningful way.

If, by contrast, the Court took the opposite approach and required universities to adopt purportedly race-neutral alternatives to racial preference, as the Bush administration urged, the winks and nods and camouflages would be even less transparent. Faced with lower-court decisions or voter referenda prohibiting the explicit consideration of race, universities have lowered admissions standards across the board to achieve racial diversity at all costs. After Texas courts and

California voters banned racial preferences in the mid-'90s, both campuses adopted so-called X-percent plans, which require the admission of students from the top of their high school classes regardless of their test scores. And, in 2001, the University of California reduced the importance of the SAT I by adopting a purportedly holistic admissions procedure known as "comprehensive review." Under the old admissions procedures, half the class on each U.C. campus was admitted according to strictly academic criteria, such as grades and test scores, and the other half was evaluated according to softer criteria, including a personal statement in which applicants were invited to discuss their success in overcoming "hardship." Under "comprehensive review," the entire class is evaluated according to the softer criteria. The results of the program have been similar to those in Texas: The average SAT I score declined at selective U.C. campuses, and the number of blacks and Hispanics slightly increased.

The Color-Blind Conservatives

Justice Thomas explicitly endorsed this approach in his dissent to the law school decision. Thomas recognized that Michigan's real interest isn't educational diversity for its own sake but a desire to maintain its high admissions standards as a selective university while, at the same time, achieving enough racial diversity to satisfy the political pressures for state universities to look like America. Although Thomas accurately diagnosed the real stakes in the case, he then resorted to raw populism. Contrasting what he calls "the people's Constitution" with a "faddish slogan of the cognoscenti," Thomas insisted that "the Law School's decision to be an elite institution does little to advance the welfare of the people of Michigan," since most of its graduates don't practice in the state. "There is nothing ancient, honorable, or constitutionally protected about 'selective' admissions," he wrote, and he questioned the value of objective predictors of academic performance, such as standardized tests.

Thomas and the color-blind conservatives, in other words, believe universities should have to choose between racial diversity and academic excellence; and they are willing to undermine the selectivity of the great public universities

—as has already happened in Texas and California—in order to vindicate the value of color-blindness. But Thomas and Scalia, who joined his opinion, offered no evidence that the Framers of the Fourteenth Amendment originally embraced such an unequivocal ban on racial classifications. Nor could they, since the historical evidence suggests that the Framers of the Fourteenth Amendment understood the Constitution to prohibit racial classifications only with respect to civil rights but not political or social rights; and, in 1868, when the Fourteenth Amendment was ratified, access to education was not considered a civil right. Thomas and Scalia claim to be devoted to the original understanding above all, and their failure to offer a historical defense of their position makes it hard to accept on their own terms.

Racial Integration Is More Beneficial than Racial Diversity

Ultimately, . . . integration itself may be a stronger justification for affirmative action than diversity. An integrated student body undoubtedly adds to diversity. But so does admitting violinists, and surely there is a stronger argument for admitting African-Americans than violinists. Higher education is one of the few arenas in modern life where racial integration remains a realistic possibility. Despite the demise of [discriminatory laws], most of us continue to live, work, socialize and worship in effectively segregated settings. College student bodies, by contrast, can be integrated because they are consciously selected and are not predetermined by geography or class. Integration in higher education in turn teaches us that integrated communities are possible, and that living in such communities can break down the deep barriers that continue to divide the races. At the same time, because a college degree is essential to professional success, integration in higher education is necessary to any measure of integration beyond.

David Cole, *Nation*, April 16, 2001.

Thomas's most powerful constitutional argument is that there is no difference between laws designed to subjugate citizens on the basis of race and those designed to benefit citizens on the basis of race. Both, he claimed, unfairly stigmatize their victims (or beneficiaries) whether they are intended to hurt or to help. "The majority of blacks are admitted to the Law School because of discrimination, and because of this policy all are tarred as undeserving," he wrote. "This problem of stigma does not depend on determinacy as to whether those stigmatized are actually the 'beneficiaries' of racial discrimination." The question of whether racial preferences hurt their beneficiaries more than help them is a relevant constitutional question. The Framers of the Fourteenth Amendment clearly intended to abolish racial classifications that created a racial caste system, such as the Black Codes, which, among other things, forbade African Americans from making contracts or inheriting property. And black conservatives such as Thomas argue powerfully that racial paternalism, and the low expectations it creates, can be just as caste-affirming as racial segregation. But most African Americans reject Thomas's argument; they insist they don't feel stigmatized by racial preferences, which they believe help to break down the racial caste system rather than perpetuate it. In the face of widespread disagreement among blacks and whites about whether or not preferences stigmatize their beneficiaries, judges should defer to legislatures rather than impose their own beliefs on a divided nation.

Rejecting Judicial Activisim

In contrast to O'Connor's uncharacteristic humility, the conservative dissenters embraced judicial activism as a kind of heroics. Thomas lambasted the Court—twice—for lacking what he calls the "courage" to forbid the use of race in university admissions. O'Connor, by contrast, recognized that the Supreme Court has a limited ability to effect social change, that the demand that universities look like America is too powerful to be uprooted by a judicial command, and that the most constructive role the Supreme Court can play is to establish clear rules and stick to them once society has structured its institutions around them. If the Court is going to act like a legislature, the least it can do is to legislate well; and, in reaffirming *Bakke*, that is what it has done.

Bakke, despite its flaws, has proved the most practical way of balancing the competing goals of educational excellence, individualized consideration, and racial diversity. Still, the compromises it represents have papered over the real causes of African American underperformance, which will persist until the nation commits itself to improve K–12 education for all. Until that happens, it's hard to share O'Connor's optimism that, "25 years from now, the use of racial preferences will no longer be necessary." When *Bakke* was decided, Powell was shocked at Thurgood Marshall's prediction that preferences would be necessary for 100 years. But, as Justice Thomas noted, the academic performance of African Americans has not noticeably improved since *Bakke*, and it is not likely to improve as long as African American students are subject to lower expectations than their white counterparts. Moreover, as the United States grows more diverse during the next quartercentury, the political demands for public institutions that look like America will not fade away. They will only grow more insistent. With admirable humility, the Court recognized that it can't begin to solve our racial problems, but, by treading lightly in an area where there is no social or constitutional consensus, it can avoid making them worse. For leading the Court to this unexpectedly modest resolution, we have Justice O'Connor to thank.

Periodical Bibliography

The following articles have been selected to supplement the diverse views presented in this chapter.

David Cole — "Rainbow School Colors," *Nation*, April 16, 2001.

Lani Guinier — "The 'Quota' Smokescreen," *Nation*, February 10, 2003.

Randall Kennedy — "Interracial Intimacy," *Atlantic Monthly*, December 2002.

Lynn Norment — "Black Women White Men, White Women Black Men," *Ebony*, November 1999.

John O'Sullivan — "Affirmative Action Forever?" *National Review*, July 28, 2003.

Tim Padgett and Frank Sikora — "Color-Blind Love," *Time*, May 12, 2003.

Maria P.P. Root — "The Color of Love," *American Prospect*, April 8, 2002.

Stanley Rothman, Martin Seymour, and Neil Nevitte — "Racial Diversity Reconsidered," *Public Interest*, Spring 2003.

Lisbeth B. Schorr — "The O'Connor Project: Can We End Racial Discrimination Without Affirmative Action? Here's What It Will Take," *American Prospect*, January 2004.

Peter H. Schuck — "Affirmative Action Is Poor Public Policy," *Chronicle of Higher Education*, May 2, 2003.

Paul Starr — "The New Politics of Diversity," *American Prospect*, June 17, 2002.

Roberto Suro — "Mixed Doubles," *American Demographics*, November 1999.

Stuart Taylor Jr. — "Ban Racial Preferences, but Keep Affirmative Action," *National Journal*, April 14, 2001.

Peter Wood — "Diversity in America," *Society*, May/June 2003.

Karl Zinsmeister — "Unchain Our Schools!" *American Enterprise*, April/May 2003.

G.E. Zuriff — "Is Racial and Ethnic Diversity Educationally Beneficial?" *World & I*, August 2002.

For Further Discussion

Chapter 1

1. Did the viewpoints by Deborah Mathis and Abigail Thernstrom affect your opinion about whether race relations are improving or worsening in the United States? If so, how? If not, why not?

2. After reading the viewpoints by Dominic J. Pulera and David Brooks, do you feel that Americans are becoming more accepting of racial and ethnic diversity? Explain your answer.

3. Shelby Steele argues that whites and blacks are too caught up in blaming racism for the problems of minorities, while Manning Marable argues that white Americans deny the reality of racism. Which viewpoint do you find more persuasive, and why?

4. Samuel P. Huntington argues that Hispanic immigration is a serious problem, while Jan Jarboe Russell refutes this idea. Which viewpoint comes closest to your own views? Explain your answer.

Chapter 2

1. What types of evidence do Joe R. Feagin and Karyn D. McKinney offer to support their claim that racism is a serious problem? How does Steve Miller support his view that the extent of racial inequality is exaggerated? Whose viewpoint do you find more convincing? Why?

2. After reading viewpoints three and four in this chapter, do you feel that racism in the health care system is a serious problem? Why or why not?

Chapter 3

1. Do you agree with Ward Connerly that the government should be "color-blind," or do you agree with Michael Eric Dyson that race-conscious policies are necessary to overcome racial inequality? Explain your answer.

2. On the issue of paying black Americans for the harms of slavery, whose viewpoint do you find more convincing—Randall Robinson's or E.R. Shipp's—and why?

Chapter 4

1. Do you feel that interracial marriages promote racial harmony? Or do you agree with Renee C. Romano that their effect on race relations is exaggerated? Explain your answers.

2. Why does the Business–Higher Education Forum believe that diversity is beneficial? Why does Heather Mac Donald believe that pro-diversity policies are harmful? Whose view do you agree with more, and why?

3. Do you feel that colleges and universities should consider race when deciding which students to admit? Explain your answer, citing from the viewpoints by Carl Cohen and Jeffrey Rosen.

Organizations to Contact

The editors have compiled the following list of organizations concerned with the issues debated in this book. The descriptions are derived from materials provided by the organizations. All have publications or information available for interested readers. The list was compiled on the date of publication of the present volume; the information provided here may change. Be aware that many organizations take several weeks or longer to respond to inquiries, so allow as much time as possible.

American Civil Liberties Union (ACLU)
125 Broad St., 18th Floor, New York, NY 10004
Web site: www.aclu.org
The ACLU is a national organization that works to defend Americans' civil rights as guaranteed by the U.S. Constitution. The ACLU publishes and distributes policy statements, pamphlets, and the semiannual newsletter *Civil Liberties Alert.*

Center for Equal Opportunity (CEO)
14 Pidgeon Hill Dr., Suite 500, Sterling, VA 20165
(703) 421-5443
Web site: www.ceousa.org
The center is a think tank that favors color-blind equal opportunity and opposes race-conscious public policies. In particular, the center opposes the expansion of racial preferences in employment, education, and voting; opposes the use of bilingual education in schools; and promotes programs to help immigrants assimilate into U.S. society. The center publishes books, including *The Melting Border: Mexico and Mexican Communities in the United States* and *Preferences in Medical Education: Racial and Ethnic Preferences at Five Public Medical Schools*, as well as regular opinion pieces and press releases.

Center for Immigration Studies (CIS)
1522 K St. NW, Suite 820, Washington, DC 20005-1202
(202) 466-8185
Web site: www.cis.org • e-mail: center@cis.org
The Center for Immigration Studies is a nonprofit research organization devoted exclusively to research and policy analysis of the economic, social, demographic, fiscal, and other impacts of immigration on the United States. CIS favors a reduction in the number of immigrants allowed into the United States each year and an increase in the government resources used to control immigration

and help immigrants assimilate. The center publishes monthly background papers on immigration issues, and a variety of reports and articles are available on its Web site.

Citizens' Commission on Civil Rights
2000 M St. NW, Suite 400, Washington, DC 20036
(202) 659-5565
Web site: www.cccr.org • e-mail: citizen@cccr.org

The commission supports the enforcement of civil rights in order to fight bias and discrimination, promote equality of opportunity in education, employment, and housing, and to promote political and economic empowerment. It monitors the civil rights policies and practices of the federal government, including federal education reform efforts and the U.S. Justice Department's handling of civil rights complaints. Commission reports include *Rights at Risk: Equality in an Age of Terrorism* and *The Test of Our Progress: The Clinton Record on Civil Rights*.

Civil Rights Project at Harvard University
125 Mt. Auburn St., 3rd Floor, Cambridge, MA 02138
(617) 496-6367
Web site: www.civilrightsproject.harvard.edu
e-mail: crp@harvard.edu

The project works to provide research and scholarship on civil rights issues. Its ultimate goal is to renew the civil rights movement in order to address ongoing, significant racial gaps in education, income, and financial wealth. Since its inception in 1996, the project has initially focused on education reform and published six books, including *Diversity Challenged* and *Racial Inequity in Special Education*; several major reports, including *A Multiracial Society with Segregated Schools: Are We Losing the Dream?* and *Race, Place, and Segregation: Redrawing the Color Line in Our Nation's Metros*; and over three hundred smaller studies.

Immigration Policy Center (IPC)
918 F St. NW, 6th Floor, Washington, DC 20004
(202) 742-5600
Web site: www.ailf.org

The center is part of the American Immigration Law Foundation (AILF), a nonprofit organization that works to advance fundamental fairness and due process under the law for immigrants. The IPC is the "think tank" portion of the AILF, dedicated to research and analysis about the contributions made to America by immigrants. The policy center publishes short biweekly policy briefs on topics such as immigrants in the military, as well as longer policy reports bimonthly on topics such as the importance of Mexican workers to America's economy.

National Association for the Advancement of Colored People (NAACP)

4805 Mt. Hope Dr., Baltimore, MD 21215
(877) NAACP-98
Web site: www.naacp.org • e-mail: youth@naacpnet.org

The NAACP is the oldest and largest civil rights organization in the United States. Its principal objective is to ensure the political, educational, social, and economic equality of minorities. It publishes the magazine *Crisis* ten times a year as well as a variety of newsletters, books, and pamphlets.

National Immigration Forum

220 I St. NE, Suite 220, Washington, DC 20002-4362
(202) 544-0004
Web site: www.immigrationforum.org

The purpose of the NIF is to embrace and uphold America's tradition as a nation of immigrants. The forum advocates and builds public support for public policies that welcome immigrants and refugees and that are fair and supportive to newcomers to the United States. It publishes several booklets, including *Basic Immigration Facts* and *From Newcomers to New Americans*, and offers a wide variety of resources on the NIF Web site.

National Urban League

120 Wall St., New York, NY 10005
(212) 558-5300
Web site: www.nul.org • e-mail: info@nul.org

A community service agency, the league aims to eliminate institutional racism in the United States. It also provides services for minorities who experience discrimination in employment, housing, welfare, and other areas. It publishes the yearly report *The State of Black America* as well as the *National Urban League Institute of Opportunity & Equality Fact Book*.

Poverty and Race Research Action Council (PRRAC)

3000 Connecticut Ave. NW, Suite 200, Washington, DC 20008
(202) 387-9887
Web site: www.prrac.org • e-mail: info@prrac.org

The council is a not-for-profit organization convened by major civil rights, civil liberties, and antipoverty groups. PRRAC's purpose is to link social science research to advocacy work in order to successfully address problems at the intersection of race and poverty. It publishes regular policy briefs, including the *Civil Rights Rollback Glossary* and *Add It Up: Using Research to Improve Education for Low-Income and Minority Students.*

U.S. Commission on Civil Rights
624 Ninth St. NW, Washington, DC 20425
Web site: www.usccr.gov

A fact-finding body, the commission reports directly to Congress and the president on the effectiveness of equal opportunity laws and programs. Its many publications include the reports *Redefining Rights in America: The Civil Rights Record of the George W. Bush Administration, 2001–2004* and *Ten-Year Check-Up: Have Federal Agencies Responded to Civil Rights Recommendations?*

Web Sites

Adversity.net
www.adversity.net

This Web site advocates for fair and equal treatment under the law without regard to race, gender, or ethnicity, and opposes affirmative action policies.

Black Commentator
www.blackcommentator.com

The *Black Commentator* is an online magazine providing commentary, analysis, and investigations on issues affecting African Americans.

Diversity Web
www.diversityweb.org

Diversity Web is a comprehensive compendium of campus practices and resources about diversity in higher education designed to help campus practitioners seeking to place diversity at the center of the academy's educational and societal mission.

Multiracial Activist
www.multiracial.com

The *Multiracial Activist* is a libertarian-oriented activist journal covering social and civil liberties issues of interest to individuals who perceive themselves to be "biracial" or "multiracial," "interracial" couples/families, and "transracial" adoptees.

Bibliography of Books

Debra van Ausdale and Joe R. Feagin — *The First R: How Children Learn Race and Racism.* Lanham, MD: Rowman & Littlefield, 2001.

Michael K. Brown et al. — *Whitewashing Race: The Myth of a Color-Blind Society.* Berkeley: University of California Press, 2003.

Sheryll Cashin — *The Failures of Integration: How Race and Class Are Undermining the American Dream.* New York: Public Affairs, 2004.

Ward Connerly — *Creating Equal: My Fight Against Racial Preferences.* San Francisco: Encounter Books, 2000.

J. Angelo Corlett — *Race, Racism, and Reparations.* Ithaca, NY: Cornell University Press, 2003.

Ellis Cose — *Color-Blind: Seeing Beyond Race in a Race-Obsessed World.* New York: HarperCollins, 1997.

Faye J. Crosby — *Affirmative Action Is Dead: Long Live Affirmative Action.* New Haven, CT: Yale University Press, 2004.

Dinesh D'Souza — *The End of Racism: Principles for a Multiracial Society.* New York: Free Press, 1995.

Robert M. Entman and Andrew Rojecki — *The Black Image in the White Mind: Media and Race in America.* Chicago: University of Chicago Press, 2000.

Joe R. Feagin and Karyn D. McKinney — *The Many Costs of Racism.* Lanham, MD: Rowman & Littlefield, 2003.

Walter Feinberg — *On Higher Ground: Education and the Case for Affirmative Action.* New York: Teachers College Press, 1998.

John Gabriel — *Whitewash: Racialized Politics and the Media.* New York: Routledge, 1998.

Hugh Davis Graham — *Collision Course: The Strange Convergence of Affirmative Action and Immigration Policy in America.* New York: Oxford University Press, 2002.

Joseph L. Graves Jr. — *The Race Myth: Why We Pretend Race Exists in America.* New York: Dutton, 2004.

Victor Davis Hanson — *Mexifornia: A State of Becoming.* New York: Encounter Books, 2003.

Cedric Herring, Verna Keith, and Hayward Derrick Horton, eds. — *Skin Deep: How Race and Skin Complexion Matter in the "Color-Blind" Era.* Urbana: University of Illinois Press, 2004.

Samuel P. Huntington — *Who Are We?: The Challenges to America's National Identity.* New York: Simon & Schuster, 2004.

Bruce A. Jacobs — *Race Manners: Navigating the Minefield Between Black and White Americans.* New York: Arcade, 1999.

Paul M. Kellstedt — *The Mass Media and the Dynamics of American Racial Attitudes.* New York: Cambridge University Press, 2003.

Randall Kennedy — *Nigger: The Strange Career of a Troublesome Word.* New York: Pantheon Books, 2002.

Molefi Kete — *Erasing Racism: The Survival of the American Nation.* Amherst, NY: Prometheus Books, 2003.

Ian F. Haney López — *Racism on Trial: The Chicano Fight for Justice.* Cambridge, MA: Belknap Press of Harvard University Press, 2003.

Heather Mac Donald — *Are Cops Racist?* Chicago: Ivan R. Dee, 2003.

Manning Marable — *The Great Walls of Democracy: The Meaning of Race in American Life.* New York: BasicCivitas Books, 2002.

Deborah Mathis — *Yet a Stranger: Why Black Americans Still Don't Feel at Home.* New York: Warner Books, 2002.

John H. McWhorter — *Authentically Black: Essays for the Black Silent Majority.* New York: Gotham Books, 2003.

Fred L. Pincus — *Reverse Discrimination: Dismantling the Myth.* Boulder, CO: Lynne Rienner, 2003.

Dominic J. Pulera — *Visible Differences: Why Race Will Matter to Americans in the Twenty-First Century.* New York: Continuum, 2002.

Randall Robinson — *The Debt: What America Owes to Blacks.* New York: Dutton, 2000.

Randall Robinson — *The Reckoning: What Blacks Owe to Each Other.* New York: Dutton, 2002.

Renee C. Romano — *Race-Mixing: Black-White Marriage in Postwar America.* Cambridge, MA: Harvard University Press, 2003.

Maria P.P. Root — *Love's Revolution: Interracial Marriage.* Philadelphia: Temple University Press, 2001.

John David Skrentny, ed. — *Color Lines: Affirmative Action, Immigration, and Civil Rights Options for America.* Chicago: University of Chicago Press, 2001.

Stephan Thernstrom and Abigail Thernstrom	*America in Black and White: One Nation, Indivisible.* New York: Simon & Schuster, 1997.
Nick Corona Vaca	*The Presumed Alliance: The Unspoken Conflict Between Latinos and Blacks and What It Means for America.* New York: Rayo, 2004.
Cornel West	*Race Matters.* New York: Vintage Books, 1994.
Lena Williams	*It's the Little Things: Everyday Interactions That Get Under the Skin of Blacks and Whites.* New York: Harcourt, 2000.
Linda Faye Williams	*The Constraint of Race: Legacies of White Skin Privilege in America.* University Park: Pennsylvania State University Press, 2003.
William J. Wilson	*The Bridge over the Racial Divide: Rising Inequality and Coalition Politics.* Berkeley: University of California Press, 1999.
Peter Wood	*Diversity: The Invention of a Concept.* New York: Encounter Books, 2003.

Index